W9-CNB-698

THE FUTURE OF BUSINESS

THE M/I/S/C/ GUIDE TO DESIGN THINKING

CON—
TENT

THE M/I/S/C/ GUIDE TO DESIGN THINKING
Copyright © 2015 by Idea Couture

All rights reserved. No part of this publication may be reproduced, distributed, or transmitted in any form or by any means, including photocopying, recording, or other electronic or mechanical methods, without the prior written permission of the publisher, except in the case of brief quotations embodied in critical reviews and certain other noncommercial uses permitted by copyright law.

First Printing, 2015

ISBN 978-0-9948265-0-3

EDITORS
CAROLINE LEUNG
ESTHER ROGERS

DESIGNERS
JULIE DO
SOPHIE QI

INTRO—DUCTION

WHEN IDEA COUTURE WAS FOUNDED EIGHT YEARS AGO, OUR MISSION WAS CLEAR: TO BRING DESIGN THINKING TO THE MANAGERIAL WORLD AND NURTURE IT INTO AN EVERYDAY PRACTICE THAT WOULD BE APPLIED TO SOLVE STRATEGIC AND TACTICAL CHALLENGES.

IN THOSE DAYS, WE KNEW THAT WE WOULD INITIALLY BE PLAYING IN THE SAME INNOVATION CONSULTANCY SPACE AS FIRMS SELLING DESIGN THINKING AS LITTLE MORE THAN A FRAMEWORK FOR IDEATION: ROLE-PLAYING EXERCISES, RAPID PROTOTYPING, AND COMMUNICATING CONCEPTS UP THE CORPORATE FOOD CHAIN. WE ALSO KNEW THAT THIS SELECTIVE SAMPLING OF A 'TOOLKIT' COULD—LIKE ALL OF THE METHODOLOGIES THAT CAME BEFORE IT WITH PROMISES OF PROVIDING COMPANIES WITH THE CREATIVE MISSING LINK TO SUCCESS—TURN DESIGN THINKING INTO A FAD BEFORE ITS VALUE WAS EXPERIENCED.

THANKFULLY, MOST OF THE 'PROPRIETARY METHODOLOGY' CHARLATANS HAVE BEEN EXPOSED AND DESIGN THINKING HAS MOVED BEYOND A FAD. AS MORE AND MORE OF THE ORGANIZATIONS WE WORKED WITH BECAME WISER TO THE PURPOSE AND PROCESS OF DESIGN THINKING, THEY, LIKE US, REALIZED THAT IT WASN'T ABOUT FUNKY WORKSHOPS FILLED WITH STICKY NOTES, BUT ABOUT DEVELOPING CONCEPTS AND CULTURES THAT WOULD HELP COMPANIES CREATE NEW GROWTH AND SUSTAIN THEIR COMPETITIVENESS.

PURSUING AND ACTIVATING THESE TWO KEY MANDATES OF DESIGN THINKING IN BUSINESS ARE MORE CRITICAL THAN EVER BEFORE FOR ONE SIMPLE REASON: WITH THE ACCELERATION OF TECHNOLOGY AND THE INTERCONNECTEDNESS OF EVERY PERSON, ORGANIZATION, AND EVEN OBJECT, TODAY'S COMPLEXITY IS MORE COMPLEX THAN YESTERDAY'S. WHETHER IT'S A COMPANY OR A COUNTRY, WE RECOGNIZE THAT SINGLE DOMAINS, TEAMS, GOVERNMENTS, OR ORGANIZATIONS

IDEA COUTURE INC. 2015.
COPYRIGHT ©

LACK THE KNOWLEDGE, EXPERIENCE, AND METHODS TO SOLVE OUR MOST PRESSING GLOBAL CHALLENGES. TODAY, THE NEED FOR GREATER COLLABORATION AND MORE EFFECTIVE, HUMAN SOLUTIONS HAS NEVER BEEN GREATER.

WE NEED TO APPROACH THESE CHALLENGES IN A SYSTEMIC MANNER, AND THAT DEMANDS A NEW WAY OF THINKING AND DOING. DESIGN THINKING CAN BE THAT WAY. ORGANIZATIONS THAT EMBRACE ITS PRINCIPLES AND ADOPT ITS PRACTICES WILL BE BETTER PREPARED TO MEET THE CHALLENGES OF A CREATIVE, MULTI-DISCIPLINARY FUTURE.

THIS BOOK IS OUR SMALL CONTRIBUTION TO THAT FUTURE. ASSEMBLED FROM SOME OF THE BEST AND MOST THOUGHT-PROVOKING ARTICLES PUBLISHED IN M/I/S/C/—IDEA COUTURE'S GLOBALLY DISTRIBUTED MAGAZINE ON DESIGN THINKING—IT IS SOMETHING OF A GUIDE TO HELPING TODAY'S ORGANIZATIONAL LEADERS COPE WITH THE OVERWHELMING COMPLEXITY AND SCALE OF THE CHALLENGES FACING THEIR BRANDS, MARKETS, AND INDUSTRIES. WITH THE PROVEN METHODS OF DESIGN THINKING, I KNOW THESE LEADERS CAN BE BETTER PREPARED FOR A NEW ERA—AN ERA OF INFINITE POSSIBILITY.

I WANT TO TAKE THIS OPPORTUNITY TO THANK ALL OF THE MANY CONTRIBUTORS TO M/I/S/C/ OVER THE PAST FOUR YEARS. YOUR PERSPECTIVES ON PRINCIPLES, PRACTICES, AND HOW YOU APPLY THEM TO YOUR DAILY CHALLENGES HAVE MADE A SIGNIFICANT CONTRIBUTION TO DESIGN THINKING AND, WITH THIS GROWTH, BEGUN THE CRITICAL PROCESS OF HELPING ORGANIZATIONS TO THINK AND DO IN NEW, MORE EFFECTIVE, AND MORE HUMAN WAYS.

THANK YOU,

IDRIS MOOTEE
GLOBAL CEO, IDEA COUTURE

01

AT THE INNOVATION IMPASSE:

HOW DESIGN THINKING CAN INSPIRE THE SUCCESS OF CHANGE

WRITER /

MORGAN GERARD, PH.D

IDEA COUTURE INC. 2015.
COPYRIGHT ©

WELCOME TO THE AGE OF THE INNOVATION IMPASSE, A CUL-DE-SAC OF CREATIVITY WHERE MANY GLOBAL GIANTS OF INDUSTRY ARE INCREASINGLY FINDING THEMSELVES STRUGGLING TO FIND THE IDEAS AND INSPIRATION TO MAINTAIN THEIR VALUE PROPOSITION AND PROFITABILITY.

IT'S A SCARY PLACE TO BE DOING BUSINESS. OTHER THAN FINER FINANCIAL DETAILS THAT POP UP ACROSS INTERNAL SPREADSHEETS, WE ARE ALL FAMILIAR WITH REASONS FOR THIS HORROR.

With so many companies making the same things, the secret to differentiation is not in the product. With more consumers making healthier, more conscientious choices than ever before, many stalwart brands that once found a place in every household now find themselves on consumer shit lists. With Netflix, Amazon, and mobile counterparts of cable giants replacing the glow of family TV time, fewer consumers are exposed to the ads that once shaped purchase decisions. With social media making it easy to spread the word, telling others about our good and bad experiences can make or break a brand.

In response to these and other disruptions to the proscriptive, top-down way that most companies have conducted business since the 1950s, the supposed fix-it to such proposition and profit woes is innovation. If only our company could learn to be more innovative, they say, we could develop product and service ideas that would drive meaningful differentiation and exponential growth.

For many such companies, the first step towards becoming more innovative is to implement sweeping title changes across the organization. Believing that if you say it you will do it, the director of marketing becomes the director of marketing innovation and, *voilà*, everything begins falling into place, right? Wrong.

What might have started as a fast one to convince *The Street* that your company has a rejuvenated approach to developing profitable ideas usually digresses into doing business the same way as you always have: The same old market research, segmentation models, packaging tweaks, line extensions, and desperation to find a Reason to Believe. The results, of course, are the same old results.

Once those results kick in, the second step is hiring innovation consultants to do most of the innovation work for you. Here, the hope is that those unencumbered by the same old habits will point the way to new processes and practices that lead to winning ideas and, along the way, provide your team with the capabilities to help your organization become innovative.

IDEA COUTURE INC. 2015. COPYRIGHT ©

GOOD IDEAS ARE LIKE ASSHOLES AND ELBOWS—MOST OF US HAVE ONE OR TWO OF THEM. INSTEAD, THE CHALLENGE LIES IN SUCCESSFULLY APPLYING THE GOOD IDEAS YOUR TEAM MIGHT COME UP WITH TO FIT THE SOCIAL AND STRUCTURAL DNA OF YOUR COMPANY.

But it's not really about having good ideas. Good ideas are like assholes and elbows—most of us have one or two of them. Instead, the challenge lies in successfully applying the good ideas your team might come up with to fit the social and structural DNA of your company.

From helping navigate cross-silo politics of participation and ownership to recognizing, appreciating, and designing for the realities of manufacturing and supply chain, any innovation consultancy worth its blended rate is adept at helping you shepherd ideas through your organization. Those that are not are just good at coming up with ideas.

It's also not really about processes and practices. If you Google "innovation process" or "innovation methodology," you'll come up with some combination of the process used by any innovation consultancy in the world. Google just a little bit deeper and you will discover all the definitions and instructions for conducting user-centered research, engaging in sensemaking, the value of rapid prototyping, and other modules of the innovation work stream.

THAT INNOVATION INDEPENDENCE WILL DEVELOP ONLY IF ORGANIZATIONS EMBRACE WHAT I ARGUE IS THE MOST CRITICAL COMPONENT OF A CULTURE OF INNOVATION: PRINCIPLES.

IDEA COUTURE INC. 2015. COPYRIGHT ©

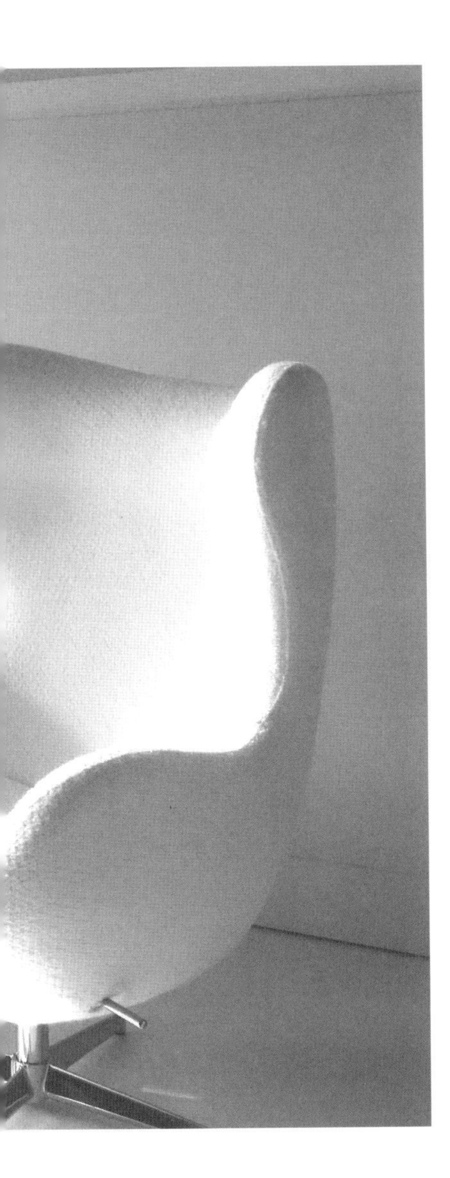

Applying those definitions and instructions after internet research is probably about as wise as self-diagnosing on WebMD. Plus, there's the fact that the day-to-day duties of the job make learning and applying new processes or practices yet another set of day-to-day duties on the job. Having consultants teach by doing is an obvious remedy, but be wary of motivations. The goal of a good partner should be to help your team foster innovation independence. That innovation independence will develop only if organizations embrace what I argue is the most critical component of a culture of innovation: principles.

While there are some pretty mercenary innovation consultancies out there whose bottom line thrives on ideas generated through applying processes and practices alone, those that subscribe to design thinking and its principles continue to lead the way because they accept one simple truth—the success of any innovation is at the mercy of human experience, expectation, behavior, and culture. Here is one simple design thinking principle: We design for people who have real needs, and the best ideas that come out of the innovation pipeline will have been designed to serve those people and their needs. If that sounds like a principle that is too radical for many large companies to swallow, that's because it is. Hence their failure to truly innovate.

What many such large companies fail to appreciate is that they are filled with people who have their own needs, one of which is to be successful at their job. Design thinking teaches us that when researching and developing ideas, we must remain cognizant of the networked relationships between and the needs of all people in a system, including employees.

If a large company takes those first few steps towards adopting a human-centric approach to innovation and includes its employees in those steps, the result can be just what is required in this scary age of doing business: inspiration. When employees, including executives, realize that innovation has a purpose beyond the meaningful differentiation and exponential growth that we all talk about—serving human needs—that inspiration can manifest and be harnessed to begin the most challenging and inventive work required to make a company more innovative: internal transformation.

If you take a human-centric approach to innovation, you realize that some of the orthodox business methodologies that have been used to identify opportunities for decades lose value. Of these, none is more inhumane than market research. Market research leads companies to talk about consumers (not people) or, worse yet, targets. It sequesters us in focus groups to "study" us for actionable insights. It puts us into segments or describes us with personas, both of which reinforce the institutional illusion that there is a real understanding of our lives. And with all the rubbish agency talk of deep dives and 360 degree views, it makes companies feel like due research diligence has been followed. It hasn't.

If you take a human-centric approach to innovation, you will energize employees. My favorite CEO—and she knows who she is—is a true champion of employee energy. Inspired by deep principles and a purpose that speaks to connecting with customers in a real, emotional human way, she has not only achieved fantastic financial results but also inspired her employees to tap into their creative energy and develop innovative ideas that lead her industry.

DESIGN THINKING TEACHES US THAT WHEN RESEARCHING AND DEVELOPING IDEAS, WE MUST REMAIN COGNIZANT OF THE NETWORKED RELATIONSHIPS BETWEEN AND THE NEEDS OF ALL PEOPLE IN A SYSTEM, INCLUDING EMPLOYEES.

IDEA COUTURE INC. 2015.
COPYRIGHT ©

INTERNAL TRANS—FOR—MATION

If you take a human-centric approach to innovation, your company will be one step closer to innovation independence. Roger Martin, the dean of the Rotman School of Management, has a great quote that I use when speaking at executive offsites: "Data is no substitute for intimacy." What he's saying is no different from what I am suggesting: If you know people and have a relationship with them, you will know what products and services will best fulfill their human needs and, in the process, meet your business objectives.

If you enjoy the scary sensation of doing business at the innovation impasse, by all means stick to that proscriptive, top-down 1950s business model you are still running. If not, consider how instilling real principles and purpose can inspire your employees and your organization to think better, do better, and be better for everyone in the network.

02

WHAT DO WE NEED MORE?

A MANAGER OR STRATEGIST?

WRITER /

IDRIS MOOTEE

IDEA COUTURE INC. 2015. COPYRIGHT ©

WE TEACH IN BUSINESS SCHOOL THE DIFFERENCE BETWEEN A GOOD DECISION AND A BAD ONE. WE TEACH STUDENTS HOW TO LEVERAGE A GOOD DECISION TO GET THE MOST OUT OF IT. WE ALSO TEACH THEM THE BEST DECISIONS ARE THOSE THAT MINIMIZE RISK AND PRODUCE THE HIGHEST RETURN. ALL TRUE, BUT MANAGEMENT DECISION-MAKING IS REALLY NOT THAT SIMPLE.

We want managers to have vision for the long term, and yet be flexible enough to respond to competition. We want them to produce consistent results, and yet experiment with innovative ideas for growth. In short, we want both change and stability. For managers, the route of stability is preferable; most of their energy and resources are spent on optimizing existing core business operations rather than preparing for change. Yet the future remains rife with uncertainties, and we remain devoid of theories that neatly packages that balance of stability and anticipation. What a good or bad decision is depends entirely on whether the decision-maker is acting as manager or strategist.

We don't really understand why companies fail. We can rationalize all their wrong moves, analyze the management's response time, or their inability to act at all. It could be that they were too slow to transform their organization when value is shifting to other activities; sometimes it's betting on new things at the cost of protecting the core. It is not unreasonable to put some of the blame on the rate of change caused by technological disruption. Management development has not significantly progressed over the past 30 years, despite the rest of the world evolving to a now virtually unrecognizable zeitgeist. We produce tons of MBAs every year—estimated at over 150,000 in the US alone and over 375,000 globally. Managers and consultants spent time analyzing mountains of data and building spreadsheets that can be used as wallpaper. Derived from them are assumptions galore, of which decisions are supposed to—or hoped to—reveal themselves. No one is capable or willing to make any decision at all. Does that sound familiar?

YET THE FUTURE REMAINS RIFE WITH UNCERTAINTIES, AND WE REMAIN DEVOID OF THEORIES THAT NEATLY PACKAGES THAT BALANCE OF STABILITY AND ANTICIPATION.

STA—
BILITY

IDEA COUTURE INC. 2015. COPYRIGHT ©

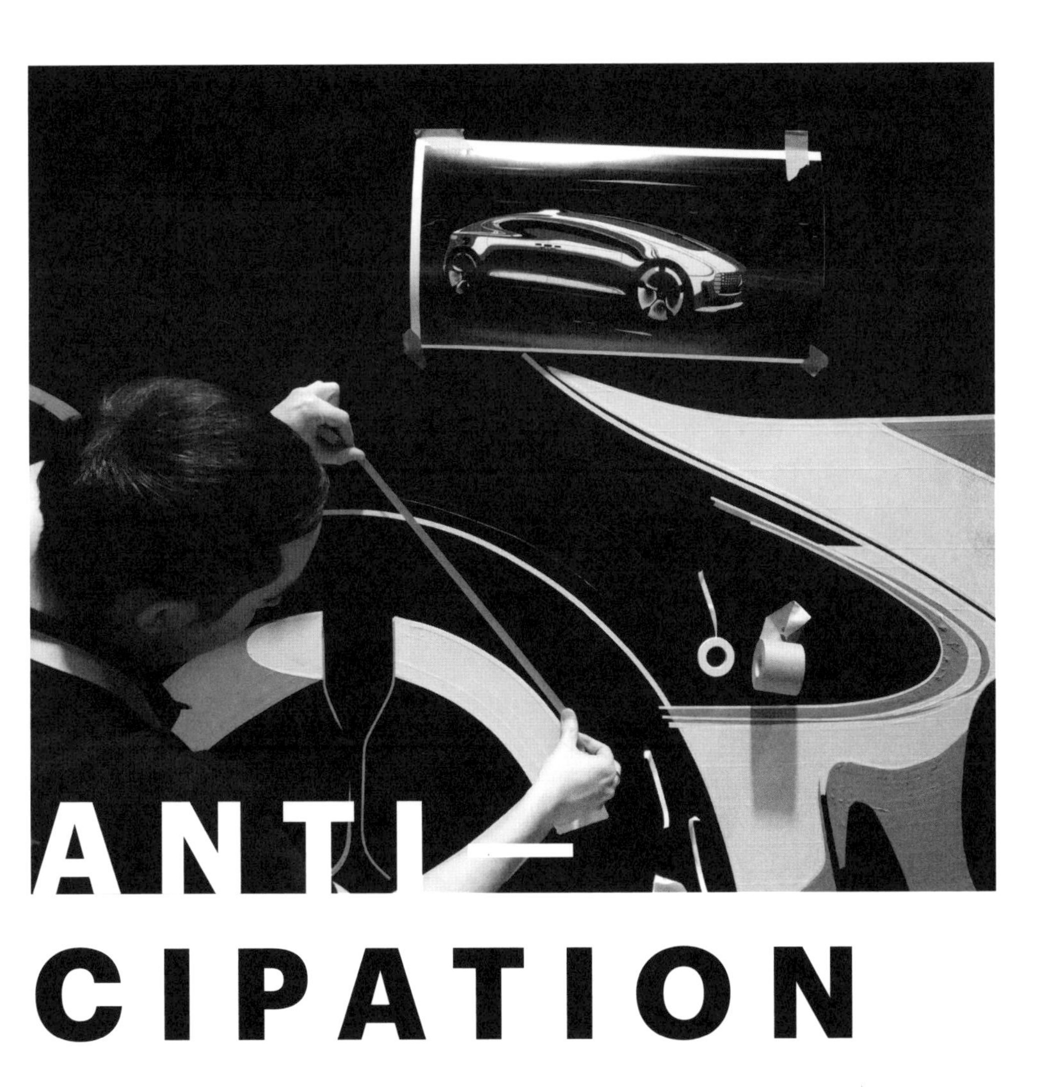

ANTI— CIPATION

Under the current business climate, we're more and more accepting that management needs to be in a risk-avoidance mode as career-protection plan. Managers operate in fear and abandon their imagination and empathy before heading to work. The strategy to success is to avoid blame and taking credit when things go right. We have forgotten that managers are hired to take risks, when in fact, that's what the best managers do—taking calculated risks and developing strategies to encourage others to do the same.

For the strategist, the only true way to maintain a useful level of predictability is to actively engage in the shaping of the organization's future. Through conceptualization and development of forward-looking scenarios, an organization can equip and prepare itself for the inevitable future.

Our emphasis on education and management development has been on training managers more than training strategists. Today, we need strategy more than ever. Our top managers need to convert to strategy. We need to empower mid and senior managers with reasons to take bolder risks, becoming the innovation force to out-strategize competition. The practice of management needs to move into a new relationship with managers and employees to move away from purely avoiding risks, to better understanding and mastering them—enabling the development of business opportunities and value creation. Ultimately, we need to train people who are equally versatile as a manager and a strategist. Today, we tend to rely on consultants for strategic advice, isolating managers almost entirely for operations. Let's find that balance.

/

WE NEED TO EMPOWER MID AND SENIOR MANAGERS WITH REASONS TO TAKE BOLDER RISKS, BECOMING THE INNOVATION FORCE TO OUT-STRATEGIZE COMPETITION.

IDEA COUTURE INC. 2015.
COPYRIGHT ©

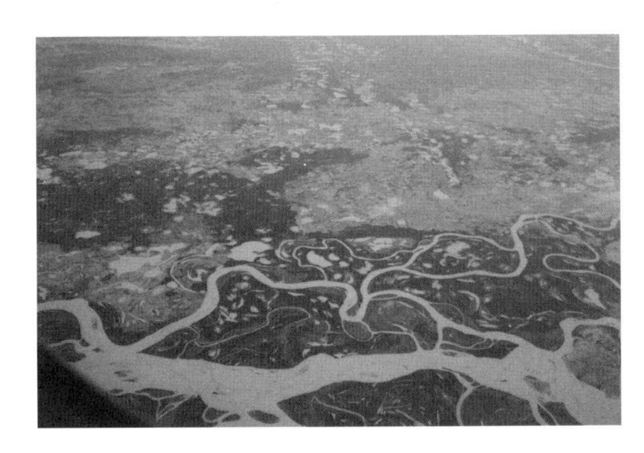

MANAGE-MENT DEVELOP-MENT HAS NOT SIGNIFICANTLY PROGRESSED OVER THE PAST 30 YEARS, DESPITE THE REST OF THE WORLD EVOLVING TO A NOW VIRTUALLY UNRECOGNIZABLE ZEITGEIST.

03

THE COWBOY VS. THE COMMANDER:

BALANCING INTUITION & ANALYSIS IN BUSINESS

WRITER /

WILL NOVOSEDLIK

IDEA COUTURE INC. 2015. COPYRIGHT ©

A MOUNTAIN HAS BEEN WRITTEN OVER THE LAST THIRTY YEARS—IN BUSINESS, SCIENTIFIC, AND POP PSYCHOLOGY—ABOUT THE WHAT, WHY, AND HOW OF DECISION-MAKING; SO MUCH SO THAT THE SUBJECT HAS LONG AGO GONE META.

The growing complexity of the challenges that we face as both individuals and organizations has fuelled the expansion of this line of inquiry and produced a body of literature so vast that there is now literature about the literature, mostly consisting of tools that will help you make decisions about what part of the decision-making literature to read.

Much of the inquiry is focused on the comparative value of analytical vs. intuitive reasoning. There is romance attached to both approaches. On the analytical side, also called the realm of "deliberate" reasoning, our romantic heroes tend to be figures like Sherlock Holmes. We marvel at their mental discipline, their ability to weave together the tiniest observations and the flimsiest pieces of evidence to produce an accurate and truthful reconstruction of the crimes they are engaged to solve.

On the intuitive side, also called the realm of "tacit" reasoning, our heroes tend to be figures who work from the "gut" and seem blessed with the ability to grasp the meaning of a situation without all the evidence that their more scientifically-minded rivals need. Faced with Gordian knots, these are the ones who slice it in half with the scimitar first and ask questions later. James Bond comes to mind in this regard.

/ IN BUSINESS, THE STEREOTYPE OF THE ENTREPRENEUR IS ASSOCIATED WITH INTUITION, WHILE THE STEREOTYPE OF THE CEO IS ASSOCIATED WITH ANALYSIS.

The reality is that these figures—and their signature talents—represent the two sides of every human being's decision-making apparatus. But despite the fact that we all possess both faculties, our historical circumstances, environments, and events tend to drive a bias towards one or the other.

In business, the stereotype of the entrepreneur is associated with intuition, while the stereotype of the CEO is associated with analysis. The former is the cowboy of commerce, the lone gun who makes decisions quickly, operating on hunches and embracing risk with gusto, not seeming to worry too much about the outcome. If the hunch turns out to be wrong, he can quickly learn from his mistakes and move on. The CEO is the commander of commerce, deliberate and risk-averse, patiently weighing the evidence until he has enough to make the call. The larger the organization, the more careful the deliberation. Turning on a dime is not an option.

The "cowboy" approach is also stereotypically associated with creativity, and hence with businesses that offer creative services—ad agencies, design firms, marketing and PR firms. In these outfits, individuals are recruited and celebrated for their ideational skills, not their research and evidence-gathering skills. Here, imagination trumps investigation. Conversely, the "commander" approach tends to be associated with accountants, lawyers, managers, and executives who are expected to weigh the evidence before committing their organizations to investing in new ideas.

But when you comb through the academic literature, what you realize is that much of the support for evidence-based decision making has been driven by the view that—contrary to the stereotype—too many managers and executives in large organizations make their decisions intuitively, not deliberately. In a business culture that has been dominated by operational efficiency for so long, this realization comes as a bit of a shock.

Ironically, this same preoccupation with cost cutting has in turn increased the pressure on creative firms to be able to predict and produce a return on their clients' marketing investments; a development that also tends to prioritize analysis over intuition.

IDEA COUTURE INC. 2015.
COPYRIGHT ©

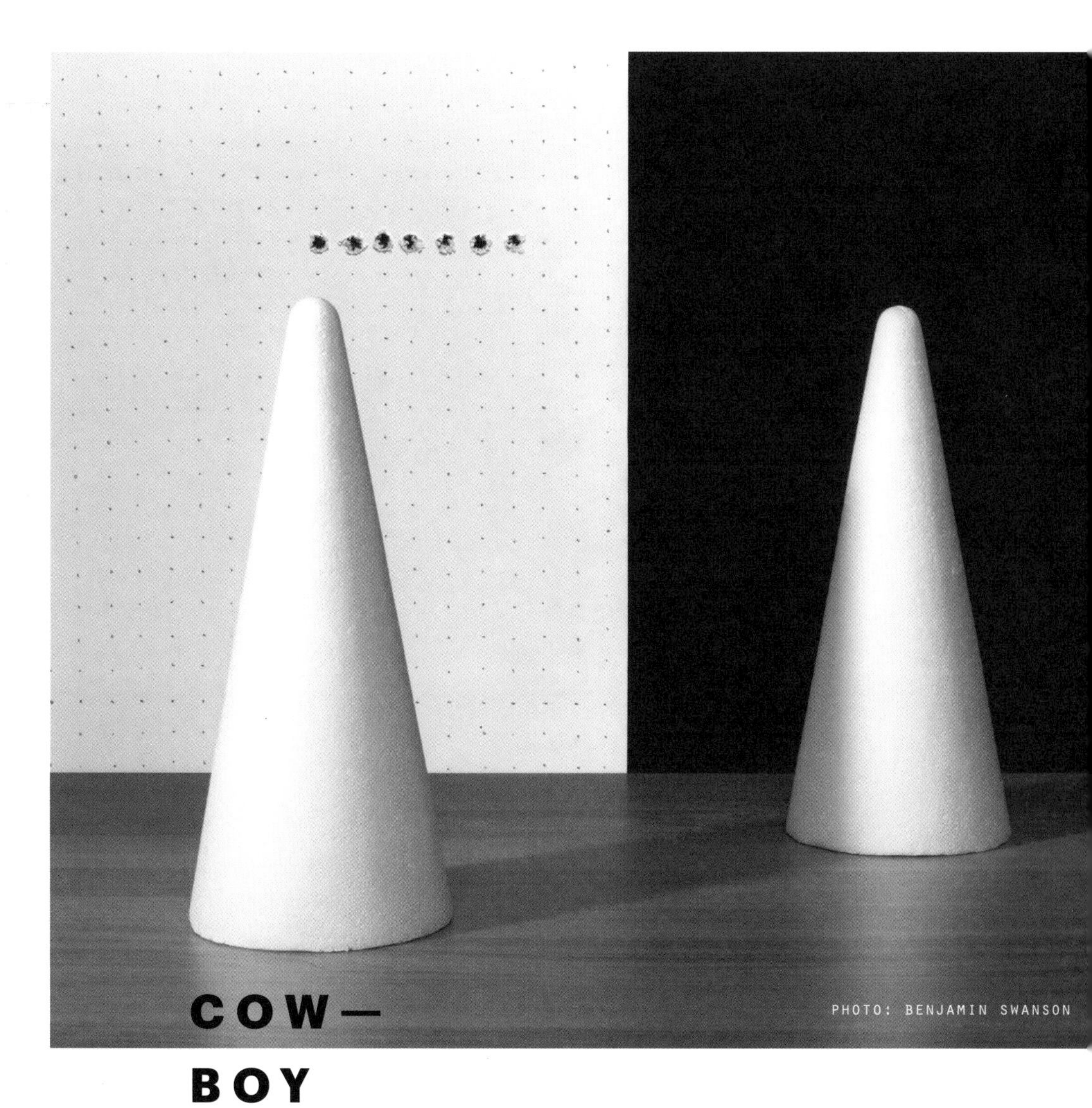

PHOTO: BENJAMIN SWANSON

COW—
BOY
VS.
COM—
MANDER

Now, creatives are expected to be more data-driven. The rise of big data, with its ability to automate the re-allocation of marketing investments towards targets that demonstrate the highest potential return, is only making this more of an issue.

At the same time, the growing awareness that cost-cutting alone is not an effective long-term strategy for competitive advantage has spawned a widespread acknowledgement of the need for innovation. Thus we see the concomitant rise in popularity of the practice of design thinking, which attempts to resolve the tension between tacit and deliberate reasoning by combining them in the same process. So now both the suits and the creatives are increasingly expected to be intuitive, as well as analytical.

As it turns out, both approaches have their place—depending on the circumstances. According to Robin Hogarth, ICREA research professor at the Universitat Pompeu Fabra in Barcelona, the environment in which a decision must be made and the nature of the task at hand are indicators of which cognitive approach is best. He argues that decisions made on the basis of highly complex inputs will benefit from tacit (intuitive) processing, and those made on the basis of less complex inputs will benefit from deliberate (analytical) processing. The environment of the former is referred to as a wicked environment, one in which feedback is unclear or not available in a timely manner. The latter is referred to as a kind environment, one in which feedback is clear and timely.

Other research supports this. A 2004 study showed that unconscious (intuitive) thought is superior to conscious (analytical) thought when the task requires the holistic processing of highly complex stimuli (Dijksterhuis, 2004). Thus in a wicked environment, intuitive processing has been observed as more effective. This may sound counterintuitive, but it has been found that the unconscious is better at determining the weights for numerous factors affecting the decision than the conscious system, which favors information that is more easily articulated and/or readily available. This validates the anecdotal notion of "analysis paralysis," which occurs when the information is so incomplete and complex that it defies logic and thus paralyzes the decision-making process.

It makes sense when you think about it. You can't possibly make an informed, deliberate decision with muddy or absent information. You need to make an educated guess—or an intuitive decision based on your experience. Since intuition is based on experience, it is affected by the degree of bias present in the environment in which the experience has occurred. It's because of this that proponents of the analytical believe intuitive processing is more likely to cause errors in judgment, whereas evidence-based cognition will be less likely to do so.

But analytical processing and a preference for quantitative validation can produce failures too. The New Coke was a classic example (if you'll

IDEA COUTURE INC. 2015. COPYRIGHT ©

SINCE INTUITION IS BASED ON EXPERIENCE, IT IS AFFECTED BY THE DEGREE OF BIAS PRESENT IN THE ENVIRONMENT IN WHICH THE EXPERIENCE HAS OCCURRED.

forgive the pun). Surveys suggested that it would be a success. History tells us it was one of the biggest marketing flops ever. So was Chrysler's CCV, the car designed for the Chinese market back in the 1990s. In both cases, the product logic seemed unassailable, and the survey data convincing. And in both cases, the results were disastrous.

Perhaps the most recently celebrated example of this line of thought is demonstrated in Malcolm Gladwell's *Blink*, in which he sets out to prove that even with all the evidence and expertise at your disposal, an unconscious clue can completely deflate the veracity of the data.

The lesson is that neither cognitive style is more valid than the other, but that their suitability is determined by the circumstances and the task at hand. The key is to know when to be the cowboy and when to be the commander. You need to balance both.

04

SERVICE DESIGN THINKING:

A CONTEMPORARY AND EMOTIONAL PERSPECTIVE ON SERVICE DESIGN

WRITER /

SCOTT FRIEDMANN

IDEA COUTURE INC. 2015. COPYRIGHT ©

THE TORRENT OF CENTURIES ROLLING OVER THE HUMAN RACE HAS CONTINUALLY BROUGHT NEW PERFECTIONS, THE CAUSE OF WHICH, EVER ACTIVE THOUGH UNSEEN, IS FOUND IN THE DEMANDS MADE BY OUR SENSES, WHICH ALWAYS IN THEIR TURNS DEMAND TO BE OCCUPIED.

—JEAN ANTHELME BRILLAT-SAVARIN

IN THE FALL OF 1998, I STARTED THE MASTERS OF HOSPITALITY MANAGEMENT PROGRAM AT THE CORNELL HOTEL SCHOOL. IT WAS AN INCREDIBLY EFFERVESCENT AND EXCITING TIME IN THE BUSINESS WORLD.

Web startups were capturing our collective attention and billions of dollars in venture capital investment. It felt like a dream, and in many ways, it was: A short-lived, unsustainable moment in our economic history.

That December, I logged on to a website called opentable.com. I made what was my first ever online restaurant reservation. There was no need to look up a phone number, no need to sit on hold, and no need to negotiate with an overwhelmed reservationist who was trained in the art of refusal. Making a reservation BOP (before OpenTable) was painful, and in direct contrast with the restaurant experience it was supposed to enable. Then along came this new tool and the ability to browse restaurant menus alongside their table inventory. Your dinner plans were secured with the click of a button and a few easy steps. Behind the scenes, OpenTable provided restaurants with a new way to sell their perishable inventory, learn about their customers, and manage their dining rooms.

While the functional task of making a reservation was made infinitely easier, the emotional outcome for consumers was more notable. Suddenly, anybody could play the role of four-star hotel concierge and master the art of the dinner reservation. And with it, a new era in service design emerged. Even moments of disappointment were met with brilliant recoveries. Suppose restaurant Jean-Georges was unavailable; OpenTable redirected disappointment with a host of other restaurant options, integrated user reviews, used points as an incentive, and built community. They mastered the art of the transaction with the emotional outcome that should have been consistent with fabulous fine dining experiences. And then they scaled the platform, globalized it, monopolized it, and sold it for $2.6 billion to Priceline.com, another service design innovator.

As an aficionado of exceptional real world service, I have always looked skeptically at the technology-driven world of service design. One of my early mentors, a senior executive in the luxury hotel business, dug in his heels and swore that nothing could match the personal touch of a human-to-human room reservation or wake up call. In the early days of service design, we took an obsessive eye to designing experiences that ensured completion of a task, while overlooking moments of surprise and delight. In the early part of the century, we were more concerned with getting a person through tasks such as the e-commerce funnel than we were about personalizing the shopping experience. We overlooked the many moments of disappointment. What happened when an item was out of stock, or in the case of an airline flight when the price increased in the middle of a transaction? Sadly, not much!

IN THE EARLY DAYS OF SERVICE DESIGN, WE TOOK AN OBSESSIVE EYE TO DESIGNING EXPERIENCES THAT ENSURED COMPLETION OF A TASK, WHILE OVERLOOKING MOMENTS OF SURPRISE AND DELIGHT.

IDEA COUTURE INC. 2015.
COPYRIGHT ©

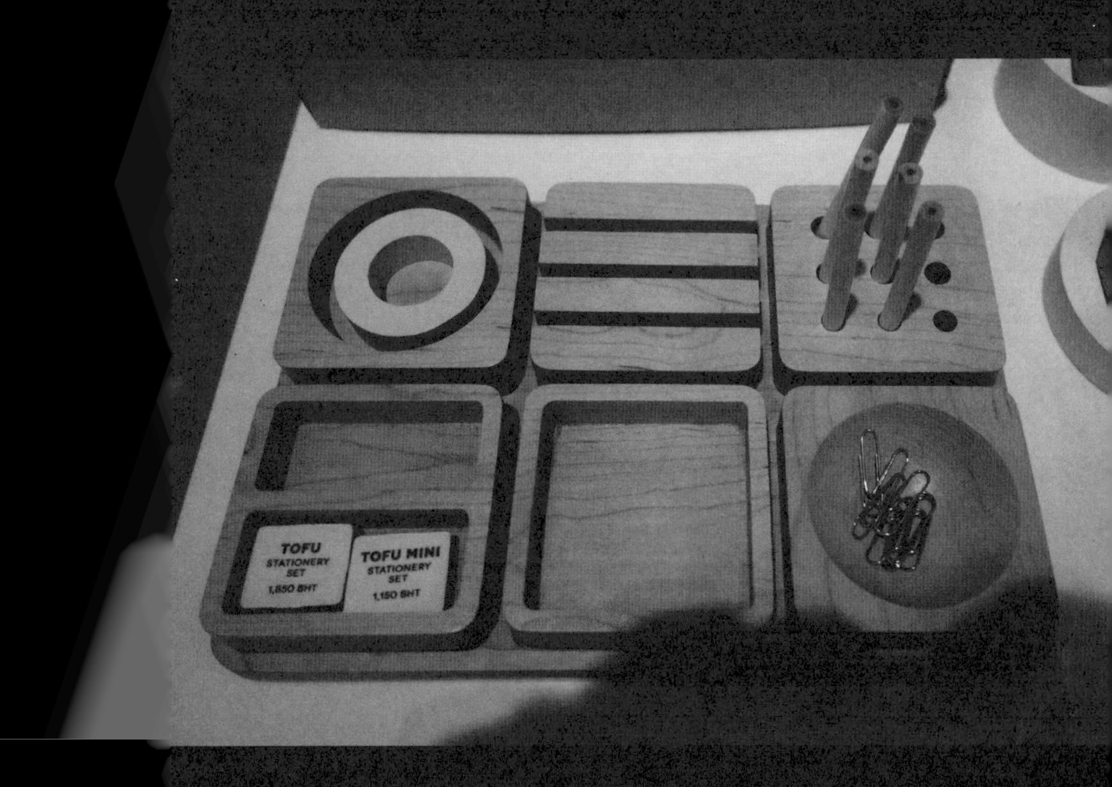

DENLY, ANYBODY COULD PLAY
OF FOUR-STAR HOTEL
ERGE AND MASTER THE ART OF

FRAMING THE DECISION PROCESS AS "SOLVING A PROBLEM" ASSUMES THAT WE AS CUSTOMERS ARE "RATIONAL PLAYERS" IN THE EXCHANGE.

Part of the problem was that we didn't have the ability to creatively make use of all the data. But a bigger part of the problem was that we couldn't engineer the spontaneity of real world service. We couldn't offer the customer a glass of champagne because we made them wait 25 minutes for their table. We couldn't walk them over to a different pair of shoes that were in stock in their size, or suggest an alternative beach that was nicer than the one with the hotel that was sold out. We couldn't manage disappointment. We couldn't map the analogue to the digital. We didn't see the need because we were obsessed with the efficiencies and profits that technology-driven service design enabled.

IDEA COUTURE INC. 2015. COPYRIGHT ©

Not that long ago, we struggled to collect enough data to make smart decisions and guide the design of services. Today, we have an overabundance of data that provides us with the opportunity to develop services that make sense of all this data. Whether it is the connected home, the connected self, the connected company, or the connected community, we need to look for new ways to combine the physical and the digital to build new service design paradigms. The new design thinking approach to service design needs to look at behavior, style, subtlety, and code. That's not just digital code and interface, but the codification of the way people do things and what makes them tick. Understanding the emotional outcome is equally as important as the rational outcome or task we are designing for.

In traditional service design thinking, we tend to start out by defining the problem for a customer in a way that ignores the complexity of human nature. Framing the decision process as "solving a problem" assumes that we as customers are "rational players" in the exchange. The reality is that people usually act more on emotion than on rationality. We define problems based on their context and our broader life experience—forgetting that they are also defined in a grander social context involving others.

Design thinking seeks to help us reframe an interaction and redefine the problem itself. Airbnb did not seek to simply increase the inventory, or improve the efficiency of booking a room or an apartment. It also considered our voyeuristic tendencies to explore places and spaces as part of the travel journey, manifesting the experience of travel television from vicarious fantasy to reality.

Contemporary service design needs to go beyond defining goals for the consumer. We can't dictate or design the experience for them. Rather, we need to provide the touchpoints, artifacts, and services that create opportunities for the experience to unfold. This is no different than the real world experience of a luxury cruise ship or resort. We would never imagine forcing people down one singular pathway. Rather we create the conditions for people to build experiences they will remember and relish. Do we remember the sum of stories and unboxings we collect from our Kickstarter portfolio, or do we remember the transactions themselves?

CORPORATIONS NEED TO BECOME FACILITATORS, NOT DICTATORS OF EXPERIENCE.

IDEA COUTURE INC. 2015.
COPYRIGHT ©

Corporations need to become facilitators, not dictators of experience. They need to move away from the TV dinner mentality and embrace the self-directed meal services of today. To do this effectively, they need to take a design-thinking lens and gain a deep understanding of customer readiness around the expectations they bring to a service design interaction. Part of this process is not just ensuring ability and clarity around the interaction; motivation, too, must be established. Motivation is not built on transactional outcomes, but a series of emotional memories. Banks are some of the worst offenders in this regard. Rigid technology backbones, over-reliance on "jobs to be done," and risk management paradigms lead financial institutions to impose experiences on us.

In the end, creation and control of experience needs to remain with the customer. People are no longer players simply completing a goal, but owners of their experience journey. The sum of these experiences make up the relationship they have with a business and the collective DNA of the brand. Contemporary service design thinking needs to be captivating; it captures our imagination. It should be familiar enough for us to navigate. It needs to be easily entrenched into our lives, yet continually evolve in proficiency. And it needs to delight, if it's going to inspire raves from the masses. This is the omakase of service design: A Japanese phrase that means "I'll leave it to you" and derived from the Japanese "to entrust." This is the ethos that companies and creators of service design need to embrace.

AS TECHNOLOGY PROGRESSES:

THE FUTURE OF HUMAN EXPERIENCE

WRITER / IDRIS MOOTEE

IDEA COUTURE INC. 2015.
COPYRIGHT ©

IN THE NOT-TOO-DISTANT FUTURE, WEARABLES AND THE INTERNET OF THINGS WILL BE DOING THINGS FOR US WITHOUT REQUIRING ANY EFFORT OR INVESTMENT ON OUR PART, REDUCING HUMAN ACTIVITY TO THE MERE PROCESS OF ACQUIRING A COMMODITY OR TURNING OUR DAILY TASKS INTO OUTSOURCED ACTIVITIES.

Just as coffee makers and washing machines have done to take over our household activities so that we have time for TV and Facebook, how will smart and wearable technology shape the future of human experience?

Technological progress has always shaped human experience in predictable and, more often than not, unpredictable ways. However, with technological advances at breakneck speed, there is more pressure on us to humanize our experiences. We need to think about the role of technology that exists in the name of our "social" and "quantified self."

Big data is about to change everything we know about ourselves. Blending that with virtual experiences, we can no longer tell what is real and what is not. What can we call the liminal space between 'real' and 'virtual'? Wearable technologies. Internet of Things. Sensors everywhere. The cloud. The drones. We now have the power to sense, in real time, just about anything and everything—amounts of information beyond the point of understanding. We are a long way from being able to use this data to understand and optimize every aspect of our existence. In the

/ IN 10 TO 15 YEARS, BIO-ENGINEERING WILL LIKELY BE PUSHING THE FIRST MASS ATTEMPT TO CONSTRUCT FIRST-PERSON EXPERIENCE AND CONTROL OF OUR BEHAVIOR THROUGH MANIPULATING OUR NEUROBIOLOGICAL BASES.

meantime, we keep collecting and generating enormous amounts of data, which has to be stored, processed, and presented in a seamless, efficient, and easily interpretable form.

In 10 to 15 years, bioengineering will likely be pushing the first mass attempt to construct first-person experience and control of our behavior through manipulating our neurobiological bases. It isn't virtual reality glasses I'm talking about—but neurobiofeedback mechanisms and virtual-reality neuroprosthetics that offer technological augmentation of human experiences to satisfy our unmet needs for motivation, competition, or comfort. Traditional neurobiofeedback works through training the waves of the brain to function more efficiently, offsetting any imbalances and "re-training" the brain to behave in different ways. It can potentially be used to improve mental clarity and focus, healthier emotions, and sharper critical decision-making skills.

The new application here goes further beyond conditioning the brain, rather using virtual-reality neuroprosthetics to instill a sense of realness within things and people that do not exist or have ceased to exist anymore. Imagine helping an aged person have a virtual conversation with a spouse who has died, or a young child connect with a parent that passed away when the child was a very young age. Or transporting one's sensory capabilities to being in space. This idea is bigger than Google or Facebook.

Loneliness—or isolation—is the biggest problem on the planet next to healthcare, with tens of millions of people around the world in search of companionship or a soulmate, and hundreds of millions of aged people wanting someone to talk to. Virtual reality neuroprosthetics is a much better solution than making friends with your OS, as seen in movies. This could be the biggest breakthrough in the applications of technology. Technological augmentation of virtual companionship can solve one of the greatest unmet needs of mankind.

IDEA COUTURE INC. 2015
COPYRIGHT ©

TECHNOLOGICAL AUGMENTATION

—

VIRTUAL COMPANIONSHIP

—

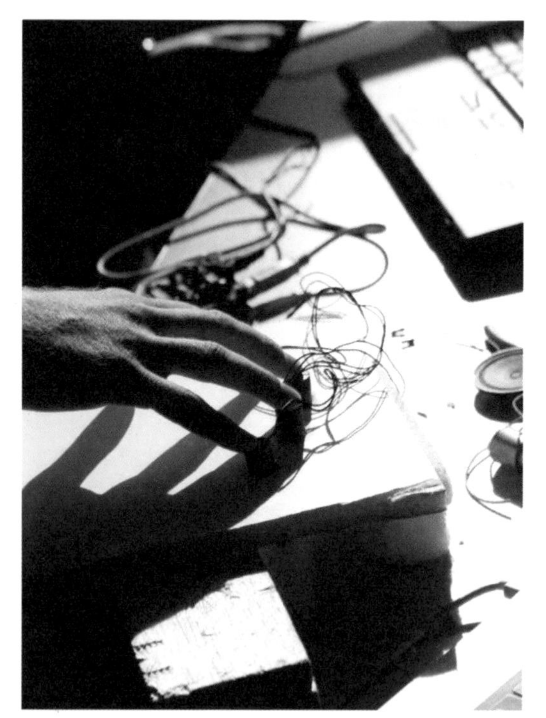

MANY OF OUR DAILY LIVES OR INTERACTIONS HAVE GONE VIRTUAL AND MAY EVEN GO FURTHER AS ROBOTIC TECHNOLOGIES ADD OR REMOVE BEHAVIORS ENTIRELY FROM OUR HUMAN REPERTOIRE.

IDEA COUTURE INC. 2015.
COPYRIGHT ©

The societies we are living in aren't quite ready for virtual-reality neuroprosthetics; we may never be. Research may be conducted behind closed doors—government agencies come to mind—but that only further justifies our fear. The potential interventions can move from prescribed medical interventions to consumer experience devices, replacing anti-depressants. The implications of a society composed of technologically enhanced people remains unclear. Advanced technologies as seen in Sci-Fi promise us futures that are intelligent and capable of improving our quality of life, but will these interventions perhaps alter the realities too much, skewing the way we live worse than any medication intervention?

The side effects for unintended use or even abuse of virtual-reality neuroprosthetics will have far bigger consequences than substance abuse. They decouple our experience from our biological bodies, and inject elements that are nonexistent. Many of our daily lives or interactions have gone virtual and may even go further as robotic technologies add or remove behaviors entirely from our human repertoire. We might even create an "improved self" by changing the way we operate or communicate, made possible only through new technologies.

Can technology improve our human experience, or will it take it away from us? The answer will depend on whom you ask the question. I was reading *Post-Process Theory: Beyond the Writing-Process Paradigm* on a flight to Taipei from San Francisco, in which Barbara Couture's essay "Modeling and Emulating" is published. She observes that writing is not merely an act that a person does to express an already formed humanity, but part of the process of becoming a human in the first place.

Writing is not something you do to express who you are; it is something that helps you become the person you will be. Reading and writing is basically a transformative act. One discovers more about themselves, the world around them, and our place in that world through a constant feedback loop of talking and listening, writing and reading.

Perhaps this feedback loop will be replaced by wearables, and that transformative act will be through interactions with devices instead of writing. Music and writing have always been the most common forms of expression of our feelings and emotions, real or imagined. Can wearable technologies be utilized beyond helping us to be more productive in performing certain tasks, expanding to emotive expression? It is really up to us to decide. Technology, like most human things, is a double-edged sword, involving gain and loss, merit and demerit. And just remember, technology is a choice—one made by humans—thus technology, no matter how efficient, needs to be human.

**TECHNOLOGY IS A CHOICE—
ONE MADE BY HUMANS—THUS
TECHNOLOGY, NO MATTER HOW
EFFICIENT,**

NEEDS TO BE HUMAN.

IDEA COUTURE INC. 2015.
COPYRIGHT ©

TECHNOLOGY, LIKE MOST HUMAN THINGS, IS A DOUBLE-EDGED SWORD, INVOLVING GAIN AND LOSS, MERIT AND DEMERIT.

06

POWERING UP:

USING SCI-FI, FANTASY, AND MAGIC TO SPARK REINVENTION

WRITER /

MARC LAFLEUR, PH.D

IDEA COUTURE INC. 2015.
COPYRIGHT ©

EVERY ORGANIZATION SHOULD BE A LITTLE MORE LIKE LUKE SKYWALKER. WHETHER IT'S THE LIGHTSABER SKILLS, TELEKINESIS, ACROBATICS, ROBOT HAND, CONNECTIVITY TO THE FORCE, OR THE JOURNEY FROM YOUNG APPRENTICE TO MASTER, THE ABILITY TO POSSESS, LEARN, AND DEVELOP NEW POWERS IS CRITICAL TO THE REINVENTION OF ANY BRAND OR BUSINESS.

For many established organizations, the inability to develop and apply new powers for competitive advantage is steeped in the disappointments of age and old habits. Unlike the heroic start-up that makes an imaginative business leap nearly equal to the surprise of Luke willing his lightsaber into his hand, established organizations may feel far too grown up to dream, imagine, and shape the world that surrounds them. With their brands' best ideas and innovations in the past, legions of employees do little more than clock in as execution engines of old principles, practices, and products.

In seeking to reconnect their organization and employees with the imagination that had so many kids reaching for invisible lightsabers post-1977—an imagination that is key to fostering a culture of innovation and design—the C-Suite pays for motivational seminars, promotes the latest pop business book to middle management, hires consultants to pick up the slack, and wonders why incremental innovation is as good as it gets. Those strategies have value, but they rarely—if ever—solve the root of the problem in organizations where innovation has become arthritic.

Enter reinvention: Powering up creativity across as many functions as needed or desired, assessing what your business and brand are today, and what they could be in the future. What are your strengths and weaknesses? What is your purpose? And is your purpose still relevant to anyone but you? Once you have come to terms with your own frail mortality, the possibilities and potentials of transformation, mutation, evolution, and disruption are there for you through the stories of your first big dreams: Magic, fantasy, and science fiction.

As storytelling genres—seen commonly through movies, books, comics, and cartoons—science fiction, fantasy, and magic function as the de facto popular media of contemporary mythology. They draw on and transmit our most powerful and popular archetypes of the hero, the wizard, the jester, the shadow, and all of those characters of our collective unconscious. They shape our sense of what we can achieve. They let us imagine what we might be.

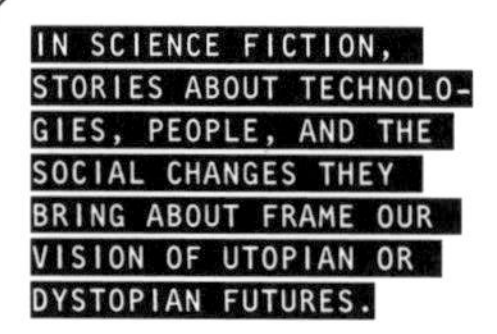

In science fiction, stories about technologies, people, and the social changes they bring about frame our vision of utopian or dystopian futures. The allegorical texts of fantasy inspire our desire to push the imaginative boundaries of what it means to be human through spectacular performances. And magic can be read as a romanticized spin on innate and undiscovered human capabilities that come to life through the incorporation of pre-technological traditions, incantations, and gestures.

Regardless of preference, reconnecting with the stories and characters of these genres can be a powerful tool for framing future business behaviors that can help transform an organization and drive new competitive advantage. For example, consider The Flash.

As if anticipating 'hyper' as the ubiquitous suffix that would permeate the atomic and space ages, Barry Allen—a.k.a. The Flash—first appeared in D.C. comic books in 1940. Nicknamed the Scarlet Speedster, he has been an iconic mainstay in the history of superheroes ever since, in part because his power is singularly easy to understand and identify with: Super speed.

IDEA COUTURE INC. 2015. COPYRIGHT ©

ONCE YOU HAVE COME TO TERMS WITH YOUR OWN FRAIL MORTALITY, THE POSSIBILITIES AND POTENTIALS OF TRANSFORMATION, MUTATION, EVOLUTION, AND DISRUPTION ARE THERE FOR YOU THROUGH THE STORIES OF YOUR FIRST BIG DREAMS: MAGIC, FANTASY, AND SCIENCE FICTION.

MAGIC FANTASY SCIENCE— FICTION

/ TECHNOLOGY IS A KEY MEDIATOR OF SPEED, BUT THE DISCOURSES AND CULTURAL EFFECTS AND SIGNIFICANCES OF SPEED ARE NOT LIMITED TO IT.

The Flash is fast. So fast, that he can disappear mid-word and return before it is completed, having run the circumference of the globe. As such, he seems to be able to be in two places at once, allowing him to attend to multiple emergencies. Using his speed and the superhuman reflexes necessary to accommodate the velocity at which he moves, The Flash can use his body as a drill, vibrate through solid objects, generate a tornado by running in a circle, become a deadly projectile, catch a bullet in mid-air, run across water, and seem invisible.

The Flash's superpower is ancient. Since at least as far back as ancient Greece, when Hermes (the sandal-winged messenger god), Nike (the goddess of victory, strength, and speed), and Antilochus (the fast running hero of the Trojan War), embodied and celebrated this power. Speed has been a prized and desired attribute of the divine and mortal worlds. As humans, we like the idea of being faster.

Like Hermes traveling between the mortal and divine worlds, characters such as The Flash alert us to the obvious advantages of speed. More significantly, they gesture towards the ways in which speed is an intrinsic facet of—if not a precursor to—modernity. With telecom providers tapping our desire for faster access on our phones by teasing us with the next G, internet providers threatening to slow download times if we consume too much bandwidth, and executives demanding shorter and faster-to-read Executive Summaries, the need for speed is shaping our lives.

IDEA COUTURE INC. 2015. COPYRIGHT ©

ENTER RE—INVENTION

While it is tempting to identify the discourse of speed as an exclusively technological one, this would be a mistake. Technology is a key mediator of speed, but the discourses and cultural effects and significances of speed are not limited to it.

In *Speed and Politics* (1977), theorist Paul Virilio refers to this dominance of speed in modern life as "dromology." Taken from the Greek word dromos (to race), he describes our fascination with and pursuit of the "science or logic of speed" as having transformed our relationship with others and the world around us. For Virilio, one consequence of dromology is that relationships between humans have largely been replaced by vast logistical enterprises that manage everyday life, thus maximizing speed and simultaneity at every turn.

Writing before large-scale processes of globalization were upon us, and long before the digital transformation of the late 20th century, Virilio provides us with a number of key insights into the consequences of speed. His central one is that dromology is not simply a discourse about time, but also of space. Here he argues that global speed entails a dramatic shrinkage of both time and space, upending traditional conceptions of space-time around which cultures, economies, and politics have been organized.

IDEA COUTURE INC. 2015.
COPYRIGHT ©

In *The Condition of Postmodernity* (1995), geographer David Harvey describes this as "time-space compression." Concerned with enumerating the particular features and consequences of global speed, especially its impact on economic production, he argues that it is in capitalism—especially our current post-Fordist phase of flexible accumulation—that we can actually witness the time-space compression. He describes it this way:

"BY TIME-SPACE COMPRESSION I MEAN TO SIGNAL... PROCESSES THAT SO REVOLUTIONIZE THE OBJECTIVE QUALITIES OF SPACE-TIME THAT WE ARE FORCED TO ALTER, SOMETIMES IN QUITE RADICAL WAYS, HOW WE REPRESENT THE WORLD TO OURSELVES. I USE THE WORD COMPRESSION BECAUSE A STRONG CASE CAN BE MADE THAT THE HISTORY OF CAPITALISM HAS BEEN CHARACTERIZED BY A SPEED-UP IN THE PACE OF LIFE, WHILE SO OVERCOMING SPATIAL BARRIERS THAT THE WORLD SOMETIMES SEEMS TO COLLAPSE IN ON US."

This compression of space-time is accompanied by an exponential increase in the amount of information we generate. As a result, dromological patterns reduce the amount of time for what political theorist William Connolly refers to as "deliberation." In *Neuropolitics* (2005) he writes that, "In today's world it is less that the large consumes the small and more that fast process overwhelms slow activity." For Connolly, one of the inherent challenges we face with the hyper production and consumption of information and communication is the increasing complexity and instantaneousness of our reactions. As this demand for immediacy becomes habitual and ever more valorized by our culture, thoughtful deliberation or drawn-out consideration become less tolerated and less valued. The result is a "tweet now, think about it later" world.

For organizations looking to increase their creative capabilities through some form of reinvention, a response to the challenge of speed is deceptively complex.

Great speed requires great energy. Unless you buy into the ridiculousness of a tenth-dimensional magical elf being responsible for the source of his speed, The Flash powers himself up through a well-balanced diet of cheeseburgers and oxygen—at least, he did for a few issues. Without them, he lacked the required kinetic energy to be super fast. To increase organizational velocity so that a brand or business can lead the pace of a market, sector, or category, you need similar creative calories.

In design-thinking organizations, creative calories are the raw materials of innovation: Immersive, human-centered research conducted anywhere other than a focus group; competitive and comparative scanning of an industry, technology or behavior; interviews conducted across the entire network of stakeholders; visual (or other) bits and bobs of inspiration; experienced, multi-disciplinary, cross-functional team members who aren't afraid to voice opinions, raise dissent, think big, and make mistakes to learn from; and a strategic framework that is quick enough to recognize and adjust to those mistakes. If you lack these internal capabilities, you will never have the energy that it takes to be fast.

Great speed also requires great vision. Where slower organizations are able to adjust navigating the road ahead, the fastest are able to see or anticipate obstacles before they appear. Some of these organizations draw on the power of intuition while others have embedded processes, such as strategic foresight, into how they map the road.

Strategic foresight is about preparing, not predicting. It is a process of establishing well-informed future oriented perspectives that fuel, guide, and inspire innovation processes, planning, and decision-making. It helps organizations better understand, imagine, and prepare for change by equipping teams with the tools and resources needed to ask provocative questions, challenge dominant logic, test assumptions, rethink opportunities, reset goals, and explore meaningful alternatives.

IDEA COUTURE INC. 2015. COPYRIGHT ©

Finally, all of these capabilities must be a part of your organizational DNA. In *A Thousand Plateaus*, philosophers Gilles Deleuze and Félix Guattari employ a concept they call "becoming" that can be particularly instructive for organizations that need to develop speed. As a process and a verb, the act of becoming releases us from the forces, grids, and boundaries that we all construct and maintain to constrain us within long-standing patterns of continuity or sameness. Here, becoming is synonymous with some degree of change, whether disruptive or incremental. More importantly, it entails a process of opening up to the characteristics, qualities, and potentials of change.

Becoming is not an imitation or a form of mimicry; nor something that can be acquired. One cannot become speed by purchasing and driving a fast car. That is a technological fix, and solutions applied on top of a slow organizational culture are not speed even if they might increase the rate of deployment or execution. Instead, an organization needs to become and embody its speed from the inside out. Like The Flash, it's not so much about moving quickly between two points and arriving first at a destination—it's about already deciding where you are going before you arrive, adjusting the course, and not crashing before arrival.

FOR ORGANIZATIONS LOOKING TO INCREASE THEIR CREATIVE CAPABILITIES THROUGH SOME FORM OF RE-INVENTION, A RESPONSE TO THE CHALLENGE OF SPEED IS DECEPTIVELY COMPLEX.

07

IN THE DETAILS:

DESIGN THINKING AND CX

WRITER /

CHEESAN CHEW

IDEA COUTURE INC. 2015.
COPYRIGHT ©

CUSTOMER EXPERIENCE IS NOT BUILT ON A SINGLE INTERACTION WITH A CUSTOMER. IT IS BUILT ON THE TENS, HUNDREDS, AND THOUSANDS OF MICRO-INTERACTIONS A CUSTOMER HAS WITH A COMPANY AND ITS PRODUCT OR SERVICE.

MORE OFTEN THAN NOT, THESE INTERACTIONS ARE CONSIDERED AND DESIGNED IN BUSINESS AND FUNCTIONAL SILOS—WITHOUT CONSIDERATION FOR THE OVERALL EXPERIENCE.

From what they read and how they are talked to, to the usability, form, and function, perception is reality for customers. It is the little things that count. Awareness and acknowledgement of the tremendous opportunities that are in the details is a first step.

A customer experience can last a second, or decades. Though enduring loyalty can't be decided upon a first impression, greatness in this regard can be. It's love at first sight—listen. Yet controlling a customer's first time encounter with a brand is less possible than we think. In general, a person first meets a brand through people threads, such as a comment on Facebook, or an overheard conversation in a coatroom. It could also happen in media threads, such as an opinion editorial in *The Times*, a post on an influential blog, or search threads (whether intentional or unintentional, or customer reviews). Brand marketing, advertising, and PR firms help organizations to establish brands in the consciousness of customers. Beyond awareness, in no part of a user journey does a brand touch a customer more than it does through its actual products or service—collectively "product." From the design blueprint of a product, to its materials and construction, packaging, and delivery, products are the physical embodiment of a brand. Experience truly begins when customers can touch, feel, and smell a product through use, interaction, and/or ownership; how it evolves and gains emotional gravity is in the in-between touchpoints outside of the product or service. Often considered as afterthoughts in product or service design, they're overlooked because they're easy to: How sexy is it to talk about contracts, invoicing, or FAQs? They are, however, tremendous opportunities to continue establishing trust and value. In designing these experiences, it's important to first understand what they are in the context of a product through rigorously mapping the customer journey at every step of the experience.

IDEA COUTURE INC. 2015.
COPYRIGHT ©

EXPERIENCE TRULY BEGINS WHEN CUSTOMERS CAN TOUCH, FEEL, AND SMELL A PRODUCT THROUGH USE, INTERACTION, AND/OR OWNERSHIP; HOW IT EVOLVES AND GAINS EMOTIONAL GRAVITY IS IN THE IN-BETWEEN TOUCHPOINTS OUTSIDE OF THE PRODUCT OR SERVICE.

It's obvious that being customer-centric is an important operating tenet for organizations, despite how surprisingly often that doesn't come across in CX. Whether in a B2C, B2B, or B2B2C context, organizations must go beyond demographics and segmentation to understand their customers' archetypes. In the simplest of cases, there is a one-to-one relationship. In others, the relationships can be far more complicated with buyers, suppliers, consumers, and intermediaries: All as "customers" of an organization, but all with differing (and sometimes competing) needs. Knowing who their representative groups of customers are—based on their shared behavior, beliefs, objectives, and needs—will help organizations design and implement world-class experiences.

But there is another side of the people equation—employees. Employees are the raw material in the world of CX. They are the energy and effort that go into making products and services a reality. Without them, there would be no experience. Any customer experience transformation must consider employee experience as a critical part of the equation. This is where the most innovative and truly magical companies tie people, process, and training together tightly with product design where the same organizational values and tenets should apply: Where CX meets EX.

From small companies to global organizations, customer experience is affected by every decision that's made. This is the butterfly effect of experience. They are those operational, people, process, and technology decisions that may start off small, but ripple through the organization, impacting customers in unexpected ways. This is where CX Scenario Planning is critical to uncovering impacts of the decisions, particularly for functional units who are two-plus degrees away from customer contact.

So why is it so important to focus on the little things? Because customers have choice, they have expectations, and in an increasingly commoditized world, the experience of the one equals the perception of the many. A micro-interaction can equal the perception of overall customer experience. Little things, over time, become big things. To be consistent and authentic in action and interaction is to build relationships, customer advocacy, and trust.

IDEA COUTURE INC. 2015.
COPYRIGHT ©

ANY CUSTOMER EXPERIENCE TRANSFORMATION MUST CONSIDER EMPLOYEE EXPERIENCE AS A CRITICAL PART OF THE EQUATION.

/

FROM SMALL COMPANIES
TO GLOBAL ORGANIZATIONS,
CUSTOMER EXPERIENCE
IS AFFECTED BY EVERY
DECISION THAT'S MADE.
THIS IS THE BUTTERFLY
EFFECT OF EXPERIENCE.

08

RE-POSITION—ING POSITIONING:

THE NEW RULES OF POST-INDUSTRIAL BRANDING

WRITER /

WILL NOVOSEDLIK

IDEA COUTURE INC. 2015.
COPYRIGHT ©

IN THE TURMOIL OF THE 21ST CENTURY MARKETPLACE, THE 20TH CENTURY BRAND TOOLKIT IS STARTING TO LOOK AS USEFUL AS A FAX MACHINE IN A SPACE STATION. IS IT TIME FOR A NEW SET OF BRAND MANAGEMENT TOOLS AND RULES?

IN THIS MODEL, YOUR CUSTOMER IS FAR MORE IMPORTANT THAN YOUR COMPETITOR, AND FAR MORE INVOLVED IN BRAND-BUILDING.

The notion of positioning that has dominated brand practice for the last 30 years has lost most of its relevance. In the early '80s, Jack Trout and Al Ries gave marketing and advertising a simple, common sense approach to brand positioning. It was perfectly suited to the brand landscape of the time. It prioritized the competitive set over the customer base, in that its frame of reference was always other brands. It was always about figuring out how to wedge yourself into a part of the customer's brain that was not yet occupied by any of your competitors. The rest of the customer—her life, her needs, her desires—were only important in as much as they could help you find your way to that undiscovered little spot in the dark corners of her cranium.

It was a product-driven approach designed to operate in a much simpler media landscape and a more limited number of communication channels. Categories were far less crowded. Markets were more localized. Balance sheets were geared towards top-line growth and as such, completely focused on customer acquisition—loyalty didn't matter too much in a volume-driven marketplace. The focus in marketing was on messaging; customer experience wasn't on anyone's radar. Marketing communications was therefore a one-way street, where brands were doing all the talking and customers could only listen.

IDEA COUTURE INC. 2015.
COPYRIGHT ©

The problem with this approach was that it was based on the assumption that the conditions of late capitalism would not significantly change. It was built on what was already there; it was not built for the future. It did not anticipate the technological and economic disruptions that were about to happen. While it sprang into existence in response to growing competitive pressure in most quarters of commerce, its key weakness was that it was perfectly designed for a mature industrial economy, not an emerging networked economy. It was like giving marketers a knife to take to a gun fight.

/ FAR MORE TECHNOLOGICALLY-ENABLED AND INFLUENTIAL CUSTOMERS OPERATING IN MUCH MORE INTENSELY COMPETITIVE CATEGORIES ARE FORCING A SHIFT FROM CUSTOMER ACQUISITION TO CUSTOMER RETENTION, AND FROM MESSAGE TO EXPERIENCE.

Thirty years later, we are in a networked economy characterized by constant technological disruption, channel proliferation and fragmentation, over-populated categories, and far fewer opportunities for differentiation. Far more technologically-enabled and influential customers operating in much more intensely competitive categories are forcing a shift from customer acquisition to customer retention, and from message to experience. They do not want to listen to brands; they want brands to listen to them. They want brands to back up their promises with action.

Jaded attitudes towards branding and advertising have resulted in lack of trust and the sharing of brand control with customers across social channels. In these conditions, traditional market research is at a loss; customers no longer want to be lab rats in front of a two-way mirror. They want a hand in making your brand. In this model, your customer is far more important than your competitor, and far more involved in brand-building.

Brand-building used to be about advertising and media. Now, it's about experience, interaction, engagement, and response. In today's brand-building, customer relationships are the lumber and customer experience is the platform. Post-industrial branding is still about occupying a unique territory on the competitive landscape, but you reach it through an intimate understanding of your customer's unmet and unarticulated needs and by crafting a differentiated experience to match them.

SO WHAT ARE THE NEW RULES FOR BRANDING IN A POST-INDUSTRIAL ECONOMY?

RE-HUMANIZE

The practice of branding has for too long been focused on products, not on people. Putting people at the center of a brand means starting with human realities, not marketing fantasies or competitive look-alikes. Put real people at the center of the branding process for authentic insights, that lead to unique opportunities for brand experiences that can be almost impossible for competitors to duplicate.

UN-POSITION

Amid a sea of sameness, brands are still getting lost in the minutiae of indistinguishable features and continuing to claim implausible emotional benefits stemming from these. In a market where customers have far greater influence and endless products that are "good enough," smart brands are more concerned with how they fit into people's lives and culture than where they fit in the competitive landscape.

NEW RULES

IDEA COUTURE INC. 2015. COPYRIGHT ©

RE-RESEARCH

Market research methods have grown tired and predictable. The effectiveness of the standard focus group is greatly diminished and increasingly anachronistic in a world of 24/7, real-time feedback via social channels. Surveys are great for making executives comfortable but are devoid of insight. As Roger Martin has said, data is no substitute for people. Today, insights require the listening and interpretative skills of the social anthropologist. Ethnography accesses the unmet and unarticulated needs that traditional market research misses.

EX-CATEGORIZE

Why compete against the other million brands in your category? What nano-niche of positioning space is there left? Don't compete with them. Compete with the whole category by creating a new one.

RE-WRITE

The language of brand strategy has become completely commoditized. Brand attributes are selected from the same list of overused, generic terms that everyone in the business has access to. Imagine every book on the shelf in your library was written with the same 100-word vocabulary; that will describe most of what passes for brand strategy today. Finding the right language to articulate a brand strategy should be just as hard as writing poetry. It's not supposed to be easy.

ANTI-REPLICATE

You still have to be different. You still have to resist the temptation to "do the same thing only better," which is what most brands try to do, and how most position themselves. And it usually amounts to a mere cosmetic difference. Meaningful differentiation is experiential. If you want to achieve meaningful differentiation, start with a real human need and work from there. Don't be a solution looking for a problem that's already been solved by a hundred others—and may not even be a problem that customers think needs solving.

/ IN A MARKET WHERE CUSTOMERS HAVE FAR GREATER INFLUENCE AND ENDLESS PRODUCTS THAT ARE GOOD ENOUGH, SMART BRANDS ARE MORE CONCERNED WITH HOW THEY FIT INTO PEOPLE'S LIVES AND CULTURE THAN WHERE THEY FIT IN THE COMPETITIVE LANDSCAPE.

WHEN DESIGN NEEDS A RESET

WRITER /

IDRIS MOOTEE

IDEA COUTURE INC. 2015. COPYRIGHT ©

I LOVE DESIGN. I LOVE DESIGNERS. I AM A DESIGNER. I TEACH DESIGN. I PRACTICE DESIGN. I THINK DESIGN.

/ DESIGN IS NOT JUST CREATIVITY. AND IT'S DEFINITELY NOT JUST ABOUT MAKING THINGS PRETTY. THOUGH THAT'S STILL IMPORTANT.

I am also the first to admit that designers can sometimes be egoistic, naïve about business and corporate politics, have zero understanding of economics, ignore human behavior or system impact, and quickly jump into visual solutions that exist outside the user or cultural context. Designers often fall into the trap of designing for their peers first, and not end users. Some see themselves as product designers; but in fact, what it is they are designing are new forms of human behavior.

Some designers attempt to cover their tracks by intellectualizing their approach, emphasizing sustainability, empathy, adductive reasoning. Yet they barely go beyond the buzzwords. As the world expects more—even magic—from design, the industry's educators are floundering for a response. What on earth should we teach future designers? What training is required? And aside from the role of designer, what profession are we actually preparing them for? While the interest in design is fast expanding, design educators are stuck on the model from the '70s and struggle to create direct relationships between design, design thinking, and much of the bigger problems facing business and societies today.

Design is not just creativity. And it's definitely not just about making things pretty—though that's still important. Constraints, consideration, and adaptability are two of the most demanding factors for creativity, while design fluency and beauty are more about taste than creativity. A designer's vision should not be overly driven by surfaces and first impressions. Instead, it should focus on the relationships among product, people, and planet. In helping designers better apply purposeful creativity, design metaphors can help designers to navigate unfamiliar design problems by juxtaposing them with easy-to-grasp and previously known situations. Getting creative concepts out from metaphors demands generative thinking; using

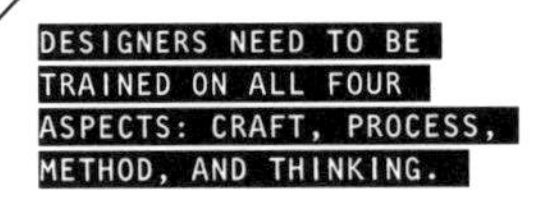

design metaphors is both a method and a process. The practicality of applying metaphor to design practice is still debatable for many, but I believe it can be very powerful when used in idea generation, channeling the thinking process through an innovative and conceptual lens.

While using metaphors can make abstract concepts easier to digest, they also shape how we think and make sense of things. For example, let's compare the smartphone interface to the vision of a DNA sequence. The DNA is shaped like a twisted ladder, where the sugar and phosphate are the rails, and the base pairs are the rungs. The rails run in opposite orientation to each other, with the rungs working as a connection between them. We can use this visualization to help design and create new forms of interactions and features on a smartphone—as opposed to the traditional grid of apps—with the content displaying much like the twisted DNA ladder, revealing different apps depending on the context of the user and the angle of the phone. In this case, we used a metaphor for opening up a designer's way of thinking, allowing them to create new interactions.

Another example is in consumer electronics. People wonder why their designs lack longevity, dismissing the iPhone's relevance in five to ten years compared to a Leica M. The average user assumes longevity as the starting point of the product's design—thus the iPhone's inferiority to the Leica in that sense—when it is the form they should be focusing on. Form is what enables the metaphor.

IDEA COUTURE INC. 2015.
COPYRIGHT ©

THE AVERAGE USER ASSUMES LONGEVITY AS THE STARTING POINT OF THE PRODUCT'S DESIGN— THUS THE IPHONE'S INFERIORITY TO THE LEICA IN THAT SENSE— WHEN IT IS THE FORM THEY SHOULD BE FOCUSING ON.

CRAFT WITHOUT METHOD IS ONLY A VISUAL EXERCISE. WITHOUT EFFECTIVE METHODS, A DESIGN PROCESS CAN ONLY GENERATE AN UN-INSPIRED RESULT.

IDEA COUTURE INC. 2015. COPYRIGHT ©

Designers need to both comprehend analytically, understanding the drivers and relationships, and be able to do sensemaking with the given information. This is often intimidating, as each new layer of design imposes constraints; how many eventually will come to light cannot be predicted. While the meaning and the language of the design does require definition and be made available to the team, design is also not an open-ended activity with a specific deadline and economic target. A designer's job is to get away from the romantic—and at times meaningless—insights that were necessary to initiate a project, and use metaphors to create hypothesis. This way, designers turn chaos to order, and from order conjure a tangible outcome that links reason, motivation, function—even adding a layer of meaning over them.

Designers need to be trained on all four aspects: craft, process, method, and thinking. Most design education focuses either on methods or process, but not on thinking. From the surface, method and process may seem like the same thing, but a closer look reveals their distinct differences. Method is how you do something, while process is putting methods through an established workflow. Craft without method is only a visual exercise. Without effective methods, a design process can only generate an uninspired result. Similarly, lacking applied design thinking means the problem can't be framed properly. The problem and solution cannot come to be without understanding the critical drivers behind them.

10

THE JOURNEY IS THE INSIGHT

WRITERS /

PATRICK GLINSKI
WILL NOVOSEDLIK

IDEA COUTURE INC. 2015. COPYRIGHT ©

WHO IS THE PROTAGONIST OF A SERVICE?

ASK THAT QUESTION WITHIN THE WALLS OF MOST ORGANIZATIONS, AND YOU'LL GET DOZENS OF DIFFERENT RESPONSES. MAYBE THE PROTAGONIST IS THE PROCESS ENGINEER WHO PAINSTAKINGLY THINKS THROUGH EVERY ASPECT OF HOW A SERVICE TOUCHPOINT IS DESIGNED. OR PERHAPS IT'S THE HEAD OF RESEARCH WHO METICULOUSLY OPTIMIZES A PROCESS BASED ON INSIGHTS. COULD IT BE THE CUSTOMER SERVICE STAFF AT THE CENTER OF THE INTERACTION? NO, IT MUST BE THE SERVICE MANAGER WHO OVERSEES THE BUSINESS RESULTS OF A SERVICE AND FOCUSES ON EFFICIENT DELIVERY THAT MAXIMIZES BUSINESS VALUE.

It's easy to understand why many organizations would respond this way. They operate from a provider-centric, "build-it-and-they-will-come" point of view. They view customer interactions within the narrow context of the transaction itself, and fail to reflect beyond what happens within their domain of control. While each of these roles may be an important part of service delivery, they are ultimately just the supporting cast. When you design a service interaction with the company at the center of the experience, the result may be functionally efficient, but it will fail to deliver any kind of deeper impact because it lacks emotional meaning to anyone not on the corporate payroll. This type of design fails to consider the customer—the true hero of the story—and the circumstances that brought them to interact with your service.

Customer journey maps are how we know the customer is the star of the story. As a tool, customer journey maps are a visualization method that bring to life a customer's entire pathway in solving a problem, including all needs, actors, and touchpoints (not to mention, the occasional interaction with your service). Understanding the customer journey is like hopping in to the Total Perspective Vortex from *The Hitchhiker's Guide to the Galaxy*. Once you're inside, you realize how truly insignificant your interaction is in the context of an individual's life. But therein lies the opportunity for insight.

These days, the best customer journey maps focus on studying brand experience from a customer-centric point of view. Putting the customer at the center of the experience reveals insights about needs, frustrations, pain points, moments of truth, and other emotional data that has not traditionally been captured in business process improvement initiatives. It helps us understand the holistic experience, highlighting unknown touchpoints and influences that we never saw from our back-office view. As such, it can be an excellent way to uncover opportunities for the development of new products, services, or experiences that will provide the emotional meaning that drives experience-based differentiation.

An example of a company that has taken the holistic customer journey into account when designing a customer experience is PharmaTrust. PharmaTrust has created a product/service combination—a remote medication dispenser—which recognizes the barriers to mobility that many patients encounter when trying to refill a prescription. Think about what happens now: You can visit your local pharmacy, or you can call for a renewal, but if you are in a position of need and are not able to access your

IDEA COUTURE INC. 2015.
COPYRIGHT ©

THE TRUE HERO OF THE STORY

PUTTING THE CUSTOMER AT THE CENTER OF THE EXPERIENCE REVEALS INSIGHTS ABOUT NEEDS, FRUSTRATIONS, PAIN POINTS, MOMENTS OF TRUTH, AND OTHER EMOTIONAL DATA THAT HAS NOT TRADITIONALLY BEEN CAPTURED IN BUSINESS PROCESS IMPROVEMENT INITIATIVES.

FROM A SYSTEMS THINKING PERSPECTIVE, CHANGING A SINGLE TOUCHPOINT—EVEN WITH THE BEST OF CUSTOMER-CENTRIC INTENTIONS IN MIND—ALWAYS HAS CROSS-FUNCTIONAL REVERBERATIONS.

pharmacy, you're out of luck. Given that most medications are for older patients, even small inconveniences can be painful. PharmaTrust took this into account when it designed its remote access kiosk, which allows you to order and refill your prescription from where you and the kiosk are—not where your pharmacy is.

Had a pharmacy considered the customer journey in this context, it would likely have taken into account only the part of the journey that happens within their retail footprint, or within a short radius of their retail location. PharmaTrust put the process within the context of the patient's life, instead of putting the patient within the context of the process, and came up with a solution that is a cross between a pharmacy and an ATM machine.

IDEA COUTURE INC. 2015.
COPYRIGHT ©

When organizations think they are the center of the story, they seldom consider the interdependencies of their decisions on the overall customer experience. From a systems thinking perspective, changing a single touchpoint—even with the best of customer-centric intentions in mind—always has cross-functional reverberations. For example, when the marketing department at a wireless operator wants to launch a special promotion, this promotion sends shockwaves throughout the organization. It needs to be managed by billing systems, frontline training in order to communicate the offer, sales need to figure out how to effectively sell it and process it properly, the finance department needs to assess the impact on service revenues and profitability, and customer care needs to know how to answer questions about the promotion. A breakdown at any of these points may have undone the positive effects of the promotion. And that customer's story is the only one that matters. The reality is most companies don't consider these interdependencies, whereas understanding the customer journey can highlight them.

The strength of the map is that it's visual; it's like the difference between seeing a place, and seeing that place on a globe. The latter makes you realize that you're part of a much bigger picture. It allows you to see that there are other places and things between and around those places that you may not have seen before. Now all is visible and the place itself can be properly viewed in context. It's something that just can't be done on a spreadsheet.

Not considering the larger customer journey is like designing a pair of Gucci loafers for someone who is about to hike through a swamp. Taking the swamp into consideration would generate a very different, and possibly very innovative design. By visualizing the experience of the customer in a way that highlights needs, frustrations, touchpoints, and influences, you gain a holistic understanding of what it's like to be your customer, and you gain a baseline for re-engineering the process under consideration. You get to walk a mile in the customer's shoes, Gucci or otherwise.

If you ask who the protagonist is of a service within the walls of most organizations, you'll get dozens of different responses, all of which are wrong. From the brand's perspective, the service is the star. But from the customer's perspective, there is a bigger and far more important journey taking place, and the service interaction is but one small part of it. Who the true protagonist is of the service story is the customer—because the story is about them.

/

IF YOU ASK WHO THE PROTAGONIST IS OF A SERVICE WITHIN THE WALLS OF MOST ORGANIZATIONS, YOU'LL GET DOZENS OF DIFFERENT RESPONSES, ALL OF WHICH ARE WRONG.

11

RE-INVENTING THE WHEEL

WRITER /

MATHEW LINCEZ

IDEA COUTURE INC. 2015.
COPYRIGHT ©

THE WHEEL IS A WIDELY RECOGNIZED ICON. A SYMBOL AND SYMPTOM OF PROGRESS, IT IS A METAPHOR FOR THE CREATION AND DISTRIBUTION OF KNOWLEDGE, ENLIGHTENMENT, AND AWARENESS; AN ILLUSTRATION OF THE CYCLICAL NATURE OF LIFE, THE INTER-CONNECTEDNESS OF OUR UNIVERSE, AND THE ONGOING BATTLE AGAINST DARKNESS AND IGNORANCE.

Once made of stone and wood, this most cherished innovation has been reinvented over millennia into newer, more efficient, and specialized versions. Each iteration applies the latest in materials and manufacturing technology to satisfy the increasingly complex needs of a modern society focused on growth, speed, efficiency, predictability, and motion. Despite all this reinvention, its core purpose—to help convert energy into motion—has not changed.

IMAGES OF PROGRESS AND THE PURSUIT OF NEW HORIZONS

The wheel has always carried us forward. The covered wagons of the "old west" and their iconic wooden spokes are widely recognized as one of the images of American progress—carrying people and resources, slow and steady over the horizon, and into the wild beyond. The wheel has been our close partner and true enabler of progress, conquest, and triumph over nature and geographies, even ourselves. For centuries, our armies, settlers, and societies have relied upon the wagon, cart, or chariot to move further and further into new territories—with greater speed and greater efficiency. The wheel has been omnipresent in our pursuit of new horizons.

Today, the wheel and its inherent symbolism of progress are no longer associated with wagon trains, chariots, and steam engines; its avenue is now the automobile. It is—as it has always been—the enabler of faster and more efficient autonomous mobility. At once, it is both a curse and a blessing to modern society. The wheel has never been more prolific. The scope of its intended use is now often adapted or reinvented as a tool to drive progress, transforming energy into motion, albeit by other means. It's an analogy beyond its material form.

Perhaps we have already reached and passed that "geographic horizon," but there are always new and as yet-explored horizons to imagine and move towards. Design thinking indulges an optimistic view that everything and anything can be improved upon, expanded, and enhanced to solve a new or emerging need, want, or desire. It remixes and plays with established archetypes, even encroaching new contexts of possibility. Now the question that remains is, what is the new horizon? What factors are shaping it? Where is the wheel taking us next?

In this resource-strapped world facing the enormous impact of climate change and mass urbanization, we find that efficiency, sustainability, self-sufficiency, and cost-effectiveness are the new needs on the horizon. And the wheel, once again, is being reinvented to take us there.

IDEA COUTURE INC. 2015.
COPYRIGHT ©

THE WHEEL HAS BEEN OUR CLOSE PARTNER AND TRUE ENABLER OF PROGRESS, CONQUEST, AND TRIUMPH OVER NATURE AND GEOGRAPHIES, EVEN OURSELVES.

THE WORLD IS CHANGING AND SO IS THE WHEEL AS WE KNOW IT

From an automotive perspective, we are now seeing greater efforts to move beyond the archetypal and ubiquitous radial tire, combustion engine, and traditional drive trains towards ever more efficient alternatives like the Layered MagWheel and Michelin's electric powered Active Wheel, which promise to play their part in carrying us forward.

Design thinking naturally takes a systems level view, examining how untapped resources and potential can be maximized by capturing and translating energy back into motion—ultimately creating even greater efficiencies. After all, the objective is to solve a real social-economic and ecological need, while maintaining relevance in a changing world and creating new points of differentiation and performance. The invention of the Layered MagWheel points us towards this new, more sustainable and energy-efficient horizon.

Conoco Phillips challenged the public to reinvent the wheel and David A. Gonzales II responded in full force. He developed the Layered MagWheel, which according to the inventor "provides powerful and efficient magnetic acceleration and frictionless regenerative magnetic braking." The Layered MagWheel captures up to 90 percent of the energy created from the friction of breaking and returns that energy back into the propulsion system instead of losing it.

This is a significant achievement in the context of peak oil and carbon reduction—as well as its obvious applications in the emerging electric vehicle market—where closed loop systems like this will lead to even greater confidence and efficiencies. Beyond accelerating the paradigm shift from fossil fuels to renewables, this development also suggests the eventual evolution towards self-perpetuating motion and truly sustainable forms of assisted mobility.

IDEA COUTURE INC. 2015.
COPYRIGHT ©

Michelin's Active Wheel is another reinvention that combines the motor, break, and suspension system into one self-propelling, shock-absorbing wheel. This approach removes the complexity, weight, and physical presence of larger combustion engines and drive train components while introducing a cleaner, lighter, more efficient and safer way to move around.

Bicycle wheels are equally iconic, and their role in enabling mobility for millions of people around the world is undeniable. Here, the Copenhagen Wheel demonstrates a significant functional shift that aligns the bicycle and its rider with the changing context of urban living. Embedded sensors inside the hub of a bicycle wheel—a nod to connected cities and the Internet of Things—transforms the wheel yet again and becomes a sensor and a data gathering mobile node, helping us become more aware of the current and future state of our cities. It provides us with the opportunity to explore new horizons in terms of the insights we gain from the analysis of big data.

REINVENTING CULTURE AND SPORT THROUGH THE WHEEL

In skateboarding, the reinvention of the wheel led to enormous growth and innovation in the sport, which now drives a multi-billion dollar culture and industry. In the sport's early days, wheels were made of steel, clay, and even wood. The lack of grip and "hardness" of these wheels made for a very bumpy, slippery, and unpredictable ride, but it was overcome by a reinvented wheel with the introduction of polyurethane. It sparked a rapid and highly creative evolution; critical barriers were removed and a latent potential was unlocked. Additionally, the softer polyurethane wheels could be easily shaped, allowing manufacturers to experiment with different forms and performance characteristics. The material properties and tolerances of these new wheels allowed people to push the limits, explore new possibilities, and pursue higher levels of performance and mastery.

RE—
INVEN—
TING

IDEA COUTURE INC. 2015.
COPYRIGHT ©

DESIGN THINKING KNOWS NO LIMITS

THE WHEEL HAS ALWAYS BEEN REINVENTED IN SOME WAY TO ALIGN ITSELF WITH SOCIETY'S NEEDS; IT DRIVES US TOWARDS CONDITIONS THAT, IN TURN, DEMAND FURTHER EVOLUTION.

Today, new wheels are being invented and reinvented to be so small, you need a microscope to see them. The rolling nano-wheel is probably the smallest means of man-made propulsion. This was achieved by a research group led by Dr. L. Grill of the University of Berlin. The structure has paddle wheels that adhere to and roll down a super-clean copper surface whose atoms are .03nm (nanometers) apart and one atom deep. The applications for this new super small wheel are still vastly unimagined and unforeseen, but allows a world enabled by the prefix "nano": Nano-facturing, nano-cars, and nano-portation.

In a similar but different world, the Hadron Collider is also playing with new scales and horizons. While not a wheel in the classic sense, the Hadron Collider is very good at transferring energy into motion. This giant wheel is helping us test fundamental physics at the smaller than sub-atomic level and has the potential to help us uncover and unlock new horizons, potentials, and capabilities, propelling us towards redefining and reinventing our world and the wheels that occupy it once more.

Specialization, complexity, and efficiency have always played a role. The wheel has always been reinvented in some way to align itself with society's needs; it drives us towards conditions that, in turn, demand further evolution. The reinvention of the wheel has always incorporated a perpetual search for greater efficiency: In transforming energy into motion, in reducing our dependency on fuel, and increasing our efficiency with resources as they become more expensive and scarce. The wheel is always contemporary. It has, and will always align itself with the needs of the society that surrounds it. It supports this evolution while also driving us forward to discover and define new horizons.

12

BY DIVINE OR BY DESIGN

WRITER /

PAUL HARTLEY

IDEA COUTURE INC. 2015.
COPYRIGHT ©

WHAT DOES IT MEAN TO
BE INSPIRED?

WHAT DO WE DO WHEN
WE ARE?

WHAT IS MISSING WHEN
WE LACK THE INSPIRATION
TO CREATE?

IF WE NEED TO BE INSPIRED
TO CREATE ANYTHING
THEN WHO—OR WHAT—
IS ACTUALLY DRIVING THE
PRODUCTION OF ART, OR
THE INVENTION OF
SOMETHING NEW?

THE IDEA OF "INSPIRATION" ITSELF ACTUALLY DEPENDS ON A METAPHOR TO MEAN ANYTHING.

When we say someone is inspired to create, we are activating a long history about the act of creation that begins in ancient thought. In doing so, we are mythologizing their creative process. And if we take a very rational view of this, we may actually be deeply insulting them because at the core of these myths lies the thought that the creative impulse comes from something outside the limits of human abilities.

To say someone is inspired suggests that they are relying on a gift from a divine, or otherworldly, source. We are saying that they need something extra they cannot provide themselves to kickstart their process of creation. The only alternative is to say that they "worked" on it, or that they "designed" it. These words describe real actions done by real people, but are stuck in the muddy depths of boring reality.

While it seems like simple semantics, the difference between "inspired" work and "designed" work is actually quite large—to say someone is inspired puts an emphasis on the creative spark. On the other hand, to say they designed something suggests their hard work is what matters. Ultimately, "inspiration" only really means anything when it is paired with the notion of design. It is a way to distinguish the products of our efforts.

There are many myths about the origins of inspiration. Western ideology locates the most impactful source of inspiration in the muses. Depending on the myth, the muses are three, four, five, or nine demi-gods who offer creative assistance to artists, scientists, and philosophers. In the most well known version, the muses are the daughters of Zeus and each is responsible for a specific sphere of artistic creation such as poetry, history, tragedy, hymns, dance, comedy, astronomy, etc.

The centerpiece of the myths about the muses was the idea that they were the real source of the inspiration and the actual work itself. Writers, painters, dancers, and scientists appealed to the muses for help whenever they were trying to create. If the seeker was worthy, the muse would provide them with the raw material to produce their masterwork. Someone without assistance from one of the muses was doomed to fail.

IDEA COUTURE INC. 2015.
COPYRIGHT ©

IN— SPIR— A— TION

/ TO SAY SOMEONE IS INSPIRED SUGGESTS THAT THEY ARE RELYING ON A GIFT FROM A DIVINE, OR OTHERWORLDLY, SOURCE.

Today, we do not believe this to be literally true, but we do speak about inspiration in a very similar way. Artists are considered by many to be inspired as they create. We talk about artists as being more connected to their emotions and full of creative energy. And in the most extreme form, they provide us with the fruits of their gifts when they paint, perform, and write. In doing so, we deny them a little bit of their agency—they are not entirely responsible for their hard earned skills.

Beyond this, when we talk about inspired creation, we see very different qualities in what is produced. An inspired artwork is more emotionally loaded. It is more beautiful and more sublime. Something that was inspired seems out of reach for "normal people," whereas something that is designed is usually more mundane and obvious. It does not seem like something out of the ordinary.

An example of this distinction can be drawn from some work I did in Istanbul examining the artistic practices of composers working in the film industry. I found that there were two groups of musicians: those trained in Turkish music, and those trained in Western musical theory. These two groups used the difference between "inspired" composition and "designed" music to explain why their music sounded so different from one another.

Those musicians who had received training in the Eastern traditions (the musical and compositional practices indigenous to Turkey) said they were "inspired" as they wrote. According to them, they write music that acknowledges a connection to some divine essence that guides their hand as they write or improvise. Their compositions are supposed to show the relatively effortless nature of the compositional process, and the melodies are supposed to be more emotionally engaging as a result.

On the other hand, those trained as Western musicians made a point of saying that they "design" their music. For them, the compositional process is simply the application of hard-earned skill. Their work is meant to be carefully composed, well crafted, intellectually engaging, and also emotionally stimulating.

IDEA COUTURE INC. 2015.
COPYRIGHT ©

As it turns out, the difference between "inspired" and "designed" was one that explained the differences in the music. The difference provided the musicians a way to talk about how they went about composing. Inspired music was seen to be more effortless because it involved improvisation, whereas designed music could be written on paper with a pen while sitting at a desk. One was intuitive. The other was natural.

For these musicians, designed music is part of human effort. It can speak to individual intellect, and it shows skill and craft—there is human involvement. Inspired music is something that is forged without the appearance of work. It is emotional and comes in an instant when one is in the moment. Thus, the process of design produces one kind of thing: Inspired creation creates another.

Now, this is a long way to go to find an analysis of what it means to be inspired, but we can take the lessons learned here and apply them elsewhere. We use the same distinction between "designed" and "inspired" when we talk about other kinds of creative effort. We design things at work. Engineers design. Consultants design. Strategists design. None of these people are inspired because what they do is achieved through the application of skill and knowledge. We generally leave the inspiration to the artists. As a result, we often mistake the fact that artistic production is the product of very hard work and that designed effort is often inspired too.

By making the distinction between designed and inspired, we make the mistake of forgetting that good work, regardless of what it may be, requires a mix of design thinking and inspired thinking. By assuming that creative work is simply the product of inspiration, we are mistaking it for something that sits apart from the effort of design. We remove the person from the picture, forgetting the process that takes a good idea and makes it great.

WE OFTEN MISTAKE THE FACT THAT ARTISTIC PRODUCTION IS THE PRODUCT OF VERY HARD WORK AND THAT DESIGNED EFFORT IS OFTEN INSPIRED TOO.

13

IS CREATIVE BRAINSTORMING REALLY CREATIVE?

WRITER /

IDRIS MOOTEE

IDEA COUTURE INC. 2015. COPYRIGHT ©

BRAIN STORM— ING—

PUTTING A FEW PEOPLE IN A ROOM WITH THE HOPE THAT THEY WILL AUTOMATICALLY GENERATE CREATIVE IDEAS HAS BECOME THE BEST WAY TO WILL CREATIVITY, FOR A HOST OF REASONS.

I'm not the only one who feels this way. Silicon Valley serial entrepreneur Marc Andreessen once posted a blog post titled "Why Brainstorming Is a Bad Idea." He's supported by David Sloan Wilson, who addresses the scientific claim that brainstorming is ineffective in his book *Evolution for Everyone*. Wilson's research suggests that brainstorming is effective only when the mental task is challenging.

Brainstorming is very difficult to manage and quality output is often very elusive. When poorly managed, the process can actually distract participants from the problems they have come together to solve. Sometimes, individuals who feel the need to prove they're right hijack the topic; in other times, the process becomes too fragmented without a proper facilitator. A good facilitator keeps everyone engaged and focused, and keeps the session as dynamic as possible so that participants are creatively productive. Once a session takes a dip, it can go off the rails pretty quickly if not properly managed.

Think of the facilitator as the orchestra conductor: The one who helps individual performers optimize their output through an artful process of discouraging criticism, maintaining the flow through salient questions and purposeful interruptions, and encouraging participants to build on others' ideas.

Brainstorming needs strategy and creativity. You need a plan, rules, tools, and the right environment for people to properly focus their creative energy. You need to avoid political traps in order to keep brainstorming from turning into "blamestorming" or "dreamstorming."

Renowned adman Alex Osborn popularized the term "brainstorming" in his book *Applied Imagination* (1953). He proposed it as a way to generate a large number of creative ideas that could then be used to solve problems and achieve objectives. His assumption was that the more people involved, the better the output, and that a team is better than one or two or three individuals.

If that's true, then "crowdstorming" would seem to be the best option. Can you imagine a town hall of 50 people brainstorming ideas? Consider the work of Paul B. Paulus, a professor of psychology at the University of Texas, who conducted research on the number and quality of ideas of four people brainstorming together versus four people brainstorming by themselves. He found that group brainstormers performed at about half the level they would if they had brainstormed alone.

A few people could get together with the right kind of wine and a great idea will suddenly burst forth. But we can't expect that to happen all the time. The biggest misconception about brainstorming is that the creative ideas and the insights leading to them are there already, somehow locked in the mind; we just need to get them out. Sadly, that's not the case.

Much of what emerges never goes anywhere.

The most common outcome is to walk away with stacks of easel pages filled with raw ideas, dump them into a spreadsheet, and vote on them. Typically there is not enough information to show if any of the ideas can be activated, and nothing is ever done with them. That requires sensemaking, a crucial step and a vital skill associated with business analysis. Otherwise, it's death by Excel.

So if the way you feel is "I went to an offsite brainstorm and all I got was this lousy T-shirt," then it's time to get creative about brainstorming.

IDEA COUTURE INC. 2015.
COPYRIGHT ©

YOU NEED TO AVOID POLITICAL TRAPS IN ORDER TO KEEP BRAIN-STORMING FROM TURNING INTO "BLAMESTORM-ING" OR "DREAM-STORMING."

/ THE BIGGEST MISCON-CEPTION ABOUT BRAIN-STORMING IS THAT THE CREATIVE IDEAS AND THE INSIGHTS LEADING TO THEM ARE THERE ALREADY, SOMEHOW LOCKED IN THE MIND; WE JUST NEED TO GET THEM OUT. SADLY, THAT'S NOT THE CASE.

14

MAKING SENSE AND SELVES:

EXPLODING THE STYLE OF REASONING IN MARKET RESEARCH

WRITER /

EMMA AIKEN-KLAR, PH.D

IDEA COUTURE INC. 2015. COPYRIGHT ©

HOW DO WE UNDERSTAND THE WORLD AROUND US? WHAT COUNTS AS TRUE OR FALSE? HOW DOES THE CREATION AND ADOPTION OF IDEAS OR STYLES SHAPE OUR SENSE OF SELF?

If you're in the business of innovation—where identifying and empathizing with consumer needs, behaviors, and attitudes drives how you design new products, services, or experiences—these are just some of the big questions you should be addressing.

Among the people you can turn to for help is Ian Hacking. A philosopher of science whose writing examines how the concept of "being" has been informed by history and culture, Hacking's *Styles of Reasoning* is a sophisticated explanation of how seemingly logical and proven conceptions of truth, reason, and objectivity are, quite simply, manufactured. Although his philosophy is primarily concerned with the creation of scientific truths in mathematics, theoretical modeling, taxonomy, and genetic development, it offers some interesting food for thought when applied to the ways in which consumer research positions itself as a practice that makes sense of the world.

Hacking challenges us to consider how objectivity has been manufactured. For him, two essential features of styles of reasoning shape how we constitute truth and experience the world. First, our styles of reasoning determine the criteria of evaluation by which they are judged. And second, our styles of reasoning create the subject matter they claim to study. What Hacking means is that not only do we invent the rules to decide what counts as "true" and what counts as "false," but we use these rules to determine what we actually study in the first place. What we conceive of as logic and truth are not actually timeless certainties—but are created by and within a system of sensemaking of our own design.

History bears this out. In mid-17th century Western Europe, the bills of mortality for the Plague of London and the record-keeping system developed for suicides in Paris led to a new way of thinking, a new kind of knowledge, and a new way of organizing the world: Data collection, probability, and the relative frequency of events. Reality and truth were henceforth defined through statistical reasoning. Thanks to keeping records on all those dead Europeans, stats are now one of the key ways we identify and measure the standards of normalcy in ourselves and the world around us. Since then, other patterns of occurrence—number of kids, income paths, sports car vs. family sedan, Coke or Pepsi—have become the go-to style of reasoning that market research uses to segment consumers, predict behaviors, and make sense of the world and opportunities for growth and profit.

As a style of reasoning that creates its own conditions of truth, market research has created new ways of thinking about and being in the world. It segments us into human categories like millennial, Gen X, or Baby Boomer. By relying on the conventions of such constructions as ways of thinking about our generational tendencies, market research attempts to parse the complexity of humanity into more manageable bits that occlude the deeper lives and behaviors of actual people. It asks us to report on those lives and behaviors in ways that self-authenticates its style of reasoning. With a dependence on surveys and focus groups to identify attitudes, preferences, or needs, market research forcibly restricts the depth of conversation that can occur around such topics. And it closes the loop on new ways of thinking about consumers through validation. By returning to the 17th century best practice of statistical modeling, market research uses the big data of quantitative testing to create its categories and craft its consumers.

Recognizing how the thinking and doing of market research is steeped in a very particular style of reasoning—one born from a plague that has since evolved to symbiotically co-exist with the ledger-like way businesses construct reality—does not necessarily discredit it as a practice. But it might help us imagine better ways of conceiving the subjects of our research.

If Hacking is correct in arguing that styles of reasoning limit what we constitute as truth, then it makes sense to argue that the mandate of today's innovators should be to dismantle our demographics, spurn our segments, purge our personas, and kill our categories. Only by challenging our styles of reasoning can we begin to create products, services, and experiences that will authentically resonate with new ways of being in the world.

IDEA COUTURE INC. 2015.
COPYRIGHT ©

WHAT WE CONCEIVE OF AS LOGIC AND TRUTH ARE NOT ACTUALLY TIMELESS CERTAINTIES—BUT ARE CREATED BY AND WITHIN A SYSTEM OF SENSE-MAKING OF OUR OWN DESIGN.

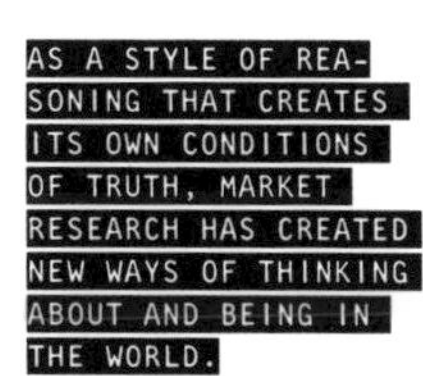

AS A STYLE OF REASONING THAT CREATES ITS OWN CONDITIONS OF TRUTH, MARKET RESEARCH HAS CREATED NEW WAYS OF THINKING ABOUT AND BEING IN THE WORLD.

15

TALKING TO STRANGERS:

THE CONVER— SATION AS BREEDING GROUND FOR INSIGHTS

WRITER /

RICHARD PALMER

IDEA COUTURE INC. 2015.
COPYRIGHT ©

AS A DESIGNER AND INNOVATOR, I LOVE A BROAD BRIEF.

I remember a brief being framed around the opportunity of helping solve loneliness in a shared social environment: How to promote interaction and integration of people who are alone, but still wish to be part of the world around them. As an individual, there are many reasons why you can feel temporarily excluded; for most, there's no example more classic than dining for one while travelling. Though not everyone wants to be inundated with interaction opportunities, I presumed that having a choice would enhance the experience. This was where I started.

On a partly filled train, I watched the behavior of individuals and groups as they found a comfortable place to journey. I placed books and newspapers on tables as prompts to see how they initiated interaction, and I watched and waited. I went to cafés, restaurants, and bars to observe what I would normally miss or ignore, and to follow conversations and interactions as they unfolded in front of me. The whole experience was interesting and immersive, but to this point not entirely fruitful.

It was only when I actually started talking to people who were alone in such environments and listening to their stories that I truly began to feel, understand, and experience the world I was observing.

Without these conversations, perspectives, and personal stories, I would never have understood the key points of insight that were the starting point for my subsequent design. Personal stories are rife with potential insights into how a future product or service could provide value, and at the earliest stage, you have to trust both intuition and interest to lead your exploration. Observation and data acquisition is beneficial in hindsight to support a theory or conceptual theme, but they mean very little without the intimacy and context of a real conversation. As a designer, it is the stories within the interaction—over observation—that provide the most easily accessible seeds of insight.

Another important aspect is the opportunity to see how these stories can be developed by your interviewee. In what ways do they imagine other people's journeys? The work by Dr. Barry Gordon and Lisa Berger in their groundbreaking work *Intelligent Memory* recognizes that ideas are created from the ability to recall and intertwine experiences sequenced as stories, and this is true for both parties in such an interview. Directly or indirectly, new perspectives and insights are fuelled by stories, not only by observations.

PERSONAL STORIES ARE RIFE WITH POTENTIAL INSIGHTS INTO HOW A FUTURE PRODUCT OR SERVICE COULD PROVIDE VALUE, AND AT THE EARLIEST STAGE, YOU HAVE TO TRUST BOTH INTUITION AND INTEREST TO LEAD YOUR EXPLORATION.

IDEA COUTURE INC. 2015. COPYRIGHT ©

PERSONAL STORIES ARE RIFE WITH POTENTIAL INSIGHTS INTO HOW A FUTURE PRODUCT OR SERVICE COULD PROVIDE VALUE

SO WHAT WERE THE KEY INSIGHTS THAT WERE SO FREELY SHARED BY MY CONVERSATIONS?

CONTROL AND PROXIMITY

When sharing any social space, there is a need to feel in control and not trapped either culturally or physically to a location where individuals whom you are not familiar with are entering your personal space:

"I HAD A BAD EXPERIENCE ON A FLIGHT, STARTING A CONVERSATION WITH THIS LADY, AND I JUST COULD NOT SHUT HER UP."

"I OFTEN SHARE A JOKE STANDING AT A BAR WHILE ORDERING A DRINK, BUT I AM FREE TO EXIT AT ANY POINT AFTER THE DRINK IS SERVED IF THE GUY IS DULL."

IDEA COUTURE INC. 2015. COPYRIGHT ©

TERRITORY AND OWNERSHIP

When entering a space or territory in a social environment, there is a feeling of ownership that prevents others from joining, or feeling invited or permitted to join. UK-based Wagamama's tables allow interaction, indiscriminately inviting all to share the same space. Patrons, however, still move in familiar huddles, claiming condiments and table space:

"WE GRABBED A TABLE BEFORE THE OTHERS GOT THE CHANCE TO CLAIM IT."

"I HATE PEOPLE WHO LEAVE THEIR BAG ON A SEAT AND THEN JOIN THE LINE IN A BUSY SELF SERVICE CAFÉ."

ORIENTATION AND SIGNALS

When you are facing someone, there is an expectation to interact. Certain repositioning or movements to change orientation send signals irrespective of their intention.

"I WAS STANDING UP SO IT WAS EASY TO JUST TURN MY BACK ON HIM."

'I JUST TURNED AND FACED MY PARTNER, BUT IT WAS UNCOMFORTABLE AS THEY WERE SITTING DIRECTLY OPPOSITE."

AN OUTSIDER'S GAZE COULD BE USEFUL, BUT A HUNDRED HOURS OF DISTANCED DATA ACQUISITION PALES COMPARED TO A SINGLE TWO-HOUR CONVERSATION.

IDEA COUTURE INC. 2015. COPYRIGHT ©

Once these insightful stories were shared by our conversations, the design task became simple, the brief became tighter, and the project progressed rapidly. The final product, a café table that encouraged and facilitated interaction, won an award. In allowing a variety of groups to share the same table naturally and comfortably, it was also highly effective at reducing redundancy in a busy café.

It's the real stories of people's lives that provide the most valuable insights. This also includes the perspective of how they see other people's lives, and what they see as drivers and motivators; often it's easier to describe your own views through the description of others. Knowing where to look and where to immerse yourself is more powerful than knowing what you're looking for.

An outsider's gaze could be useful, but a hundred hours of distanced data acquisition pales compared to a single two-hour conversation. Data must always look backwards, but insight and vision have the opportunity to really look forward. Stories based upon both the past and possible futures fit naturally into the way we understand and imagine a better world. The sooner we get immersed and start listening, the better.

16

THE BEST IDEAS WILL BREAK YOU

WRITER /

JAYAR LA FONTAINE

IDEA COUTURE INC. 2015. COPYRIGHT ©

TELL ME IF THIS SCENARIO SOUNDS FAMILIAR: YOU'VE JUST COME OUT OF AN INVIGORATING WORKSHOP WITH YOUR IMAGINATION KINDLED BY THE IDEAS THAT HAD BEEN FLOATING AROUND THE ROOM. HIGH ON THE FRISSON, YOU'RE CAREENING THROUGH NEW, STRANGE THOUGHTS. YOU FEEL ALIVE TO POSSIBILITIES. YOU SEE EVERYTHING, IT SEEMS, IN A NEW LIGHT.

The next day, the sensations you felt are dimmer. You're still feeling inspired, but you've also got a mountain of things to catch up on. There's a business to be run, after all. But you try to hold on to that sense of excitement. Something will come of it, you assure yourself. And then you get back to work.

By the following week, the post-workshop charge has faded to, at best, a pleasant, lingering buzz. You might be buoyed along during your day by a mild sense of mental well being, but the spark you felt has been reduced to an ember. A month passes, and you can barely remember the specifics of the discussions that took place, but by then—inspiration junkie that you are—you've moved on to other sources of intellectual espresso, chasing the next fix that you feel will lead to a breakthrough.

But that next energizing fix probably won't do the trick either. Here's the dirty truth that the whole industry of conferences, workshops, and publications aimed at inspiring our thinking choose to ignore: We are terrible at telling the difference between ideas that are important and those that simply feel good to contemplate. What's worse: Those ideas that shoot through us like lightning and supercharge us may be the least likely to lead to breakthroughs because concepts that find a ready home in our minds usually need to do very little to alter our mental landscape. Instead, they naturally settle into some comfortable pocket of our existing beliefs.

idea
couture

IDEA COUTURE INC. 2015.
COPYRIGHT ©

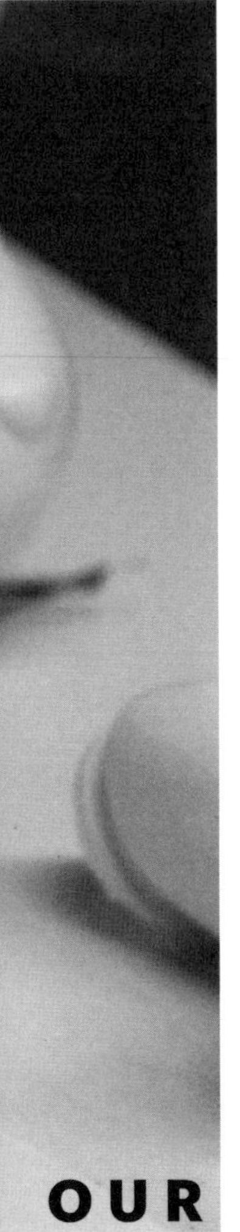

So why are we so attracted to those "big ideas" that make us feel charged? Cognitive scientists who study belief formation call it the prior attitude effect. People who feel strongly about an issue—even when encouraged to be objective—will evaluate supportive evidence more favorably than disconfirming evidence. Our minds crave confirmation, and the bigger the idea we can assimilate to support our thinking, the bigger the charge we get.

On the other hand, thoughts that challenge our mental models hurt in a way that thinking supportive thoughts do not, and so we avoid disconfirming ideas at all costs, especially the big and scary ones. Unfortunately for us, it's the big and scary ideas—those that crash into our mental worlds like an asteroid, leaving ugly impact craters in the beliefs and attitudes at the center of ourselves—that are more likely to lead to fundamental breakthroughs in our thinking.

And mental models are not easy things to break. Because of this, the condition that leads to real breakthrough thinking is more like a period of illness and convalescence than a jolt of sudden energy. Don't expect overnight enlightenment. Truly disruptive ideas create mental wounds that take time to heal over. They force us to rearrange pieces of ourselves, or even to abandon cherished beliefs entirely when they no longer fit alongside our new knowledge.

OUR MINDS CRAVE CONFIRMATION, AND THE BIGGER THE IDEA WE CAN ASSIMILATE TO SUPPORT OUR THINKING, THE BIGGER THE CHARGE WE GET.

WE ARE TERRIBLE AT TELLING THE DIFFERENCE BETWEEN IDEAS THAT ARE IMPORTANT AND THOSE THAT SIMPLY FEEL GOOD TO CONTEMPLATE.

IDEA COUTURE INC. 2015.
COPYRIGHT ©

If we want to see the protracted pain of real breakthrough thinking in full display, we should ignore accounts of thinkers who experienced "Eureka!" moments and look instead to the stories of thinkers whose worldviews have been deeply wounded by ideas that stuck deep into their psyches. Take the case of novelist Alfred Koestler.

Though he is best remembered as the author of the anti-totalitarianism novel *Darkness at Noon*, Koestler also helped to assemble one of the most remarkable historical documents of the 20th century. *The God that Failed*, published in 1949, is a collection of six testimonial essays by famous ex-Communist writers and journalists examining their entrancement with Communism and the intellectual and emotional aftermath of the eventual falling-away of their deeply held political beliefs. The essay Koestler himself wrote for the collection is both a fascinating insider's look at revolutionary activity in Russia and Europe during the inter-war period, and a stark account of the creeping pain and anguish of genuine breakthrough thinking.

Koestler's fervent worldview came together seamlessly in his mind in just the way we'd expect with ideas that confirm our prior attitudes. Becoming a Communist didn't change Koestler; it just gave him a language for deftly expressing the attitudes and "social conscience" he had acquired as an adolescent with personal experiences of poverty and injustice. For him, reading the work of Marx and Engels had "the intoxicating effect of a sudden liberation from the rusty chains with which a pre-1914 middle-class childhood had cluttered one's mind." It allowed him to become who he was already.

This language—the intoxicating effect of sudden liberation—sounds like the dose of breakthrough thinking that we expect to get from watching TED Talks and reading Fast Company. But beware: The intoxicating effects of sudden breakthroughs linger and impair our ability to sober-mindedly judge new information. Intoxicating ideas can turn our worldviews into addictions that we need to feed with confirmatory evidence. We can also begin to dismiss anything that could challenge our thinking by rationalizing it all away—or shutting our eyes and covering our ears. We might tell ourselves that our ideas are sound and that they stand in the face of evidence. But are we sure that we aren't simply shrinking away from the pain and discomfort of dangerous ideas? Reflecting on his mindset decades later, Koestler tells us, "The passions of that time seem transformed into perversions, its inner certitude into the closed universe of the drug addict."

Like an addict, Koestler was not immediately ready to admit to himself that his mental model had impaired his ability to interact with simple truths about reality. As a young writer touring the Soviet Union, Koestler's mind became the battleground for a war between a deeply held, rigid ideology and the countervailing evidence provided by his own senses, both physical and moral.

Initially, Koestler registered his experiences—of the unaffordability of basic commodities, of the ravages of famine in the Ukraine, of the sudden and permanent disappearance of friends and colleagues into gulags—in ways that fit with what he believed to be true: Inflated prices and food shortages were a reflection of the actions of Marxism's enemies, and imprisoned comrades must have been engaging in secret counterrevolutionary activity. Koestler wrote about the efforts of his mind to cope with what he saw: "Having experienced the almost unlimited possibilities of mental acrobatism on that tight rope stretched across one's conscience, I know how much stretching it takes to make that elastic rope snap."

The final irony of Koestler's story—and of the story of breakthrough thinking in general—is that the ideas that can "snap the elastic rope" and upend a worldview are often themselves drab and commonplace. The thoughts that prefigured Koestler's breakthrough came to him as he sat in a Spanish prison, awaiting either liberation or the firing squad: That humans are a reality and humankind an abstraction; that the ends justify the means only within narrow limits; that people could never be ordered like cogs in a machine because they weren't cogs. And it was only after many more months allowing these insights to marinate that Koestler finally broke his ties with the Party.

IDEA COUTURE INC. 2015. COPYRIGHT ©

IF WE'RE GOING TO PROTECT OURSELVES FROM BEING BLINDED BY OUR OWN WORLDVIEWS, WE HAVE TO UNDERSTAND THAT OUR MINDS FORTIFY THEMSELVES BECAUSE THEY DON'T WANT TO ACCOMMODATE GENUINELY DISRUPTIVE IDEAS

The American philosopher Willard Van Ormon Quine wrote, "Our statements about the external world face the tribunal of sense experience not individually but only as a corporate body." Standing alone, any one element of Koestler's worldview might have fallen quickly to countervailing evidence and basic truths. However, as a network, they lent justificatory support to one another and gave Koestler avenues of escape from having to meet reality head-on, allowing him to engage elaborate "mental acrobatics."

If we're going to protect ourselves from being blinded by our own worldviews, we have to understand that our minds fortify themselves because they don't want to accommodate genuinely disruptive ideas, which are painful and cut deep and leave lasting scars. Then, if we really want to open ourselves to the possibility of disruptive thinking, we have to learn to fight the urge to shield ourselves, as did Koestler. Breakthroughs can't happen if nothing gets broken.

17